W9-BHI-350

Drawn to Destiny

How to Discover and Bring to Fruition Your True Purpose in Life

Drawn to Destiny

How to Discover and Bring to Fruition Your True Purpose in Life

Dr. Yvonne Capehart

Unless otherwise indicated, all Scripture quotations are from the King James Version of the Bible. References marked "NKJ" are from the New King James Version of the Bible, copyright © 1979, 1980, 1982, by Thomas Nelson, Inc., Nashville, Tennessee.

Bible name meanings are taken from Holman Illustrated Bible Dictionary, copyright © 2003, Holman Bible Publishers, Nashville, Tennessee. Word definitions are taken from Webster's New Practical School Dictionary, copyright © 1969, Merriam Webster American Book Company, New York, New York.

Drawn to Destiny: How to Discover and Bring to Fruition Your True Purpose in Life
ISBN 1-880809-47-8

Printed in the United States of America
Copyright © 2005—by Yvonne Capehart

Legacy Publishers International
1301 South Clinton Street
Denver, CO 80247
Phone: 303-283-7480 FAX: 303-283-7536

Library of Congress Cataloging-in-Publication Data Pending

No part of this book may be reproduced or transmitted in any form or by any means, electronic or mechanical, including photocopying, recording, or by any information retrieval system.

Dedication

To my dear friend Eleanor:

You have taught me the power of trusting God, no matter what, as I watched you walk through a very difficult trial, while still maintaining your integrity in God.

Acknowledgments

I want to thank my wonderful husband, Pastor Lee, for his love and support throughout our twenty years of marriage. You have always given me the courage, the strength, and the push I needed to reach my destiny.

To my sons Brandon and Britton: Thank you for being great guys. Most of all, thank you for sharing me with those to whom God has called me.

To my family: Your prayer and support has always been my strength.

To my staff at Sister Keepers International Ministries and my church family at Believer's Life Center: Thank you for your loyalty and support. Your labor is not in vain.

Special thanks to all my friends in leadership who have covered me in prayer and given me godly counsel.

To the staff of Legacy Publishers International: Thank you for your guidance during this project.

Most and foremost, I want to thank the Lord Jesus Christ for drawing me to my destiny—despite the failings of my past.

Contents

Introduction

As a daughter of God, now is your time to walk in the destiny that He has purposed for your life. No matter what comes your way, no matter what circumstances try to interfere with God's plan for your life, know that there is a call upon you, a destiny in you, and nothing can stop that destiny from coming to fruition. Nothing!

It doesn't matter what your friends say or what deceptive lies the enemy has tried to plant in your heart. Because God has a destiny, a call, upon your life, He's using every situation to pull you closer to that destiny. The purpose of this book is to help you understand its existence and to draw you ever closer to it.

In my younger days, when I developed a message to preach, I would take one or two scriptures and minister on them until we all went up into glory. Lately, however, the Lord has taught me a new method. Now He invites me into

His Word as a gourmet chef, tutoring me on how to stir, simmer, and savor His revelations in a more memorable and impactful way. *Drawn to Destiny* has been birthed out of that slow, spiritual-cooking process and has come to me, bit by bit. Now I'm pleased to be able to share it with you for the first time in print.

As I lovingly serve you these revelations—bite by bite, morsel by morsel, chapter by chapter, the Lord has assured me that they will change the life of every real daughter of His who reads this book. *Drawn to Destiny* is a vessel of change for God's real daughters, daughters who have been patiently waiting before Him. As one of His real daughters, this gourmet feast of divine revelations is intended for you, a woman from the house of the Father, planted firmly in His presence:

> *Those that be planted in the house of the Lord [His real daughters] shall flourish in the courts of our God.*
>
> *Psalm 92:13*

You've been *"planted,"* and now it's your time to *"flourish."*

Dr. Yvonne Capehart
Pensacola, Florida

Part One

The Drawing

Chapter One

The Plan of Purpose

CAPEHART'S CORNER: *When it's your time, you don't have to do anything but be found!*

Favored to Be Found

Friend, have you come to accept life as an obstacle course or a rat's maze, and are you running from one dead end to another without finding a means of escape? Are you in search of the reason you've gone through all that you've gone through and somehow survived, or the reason you've had to experience many difficult days and had a constant cry for relief in your heart, only to discover that relief came by nothing but your willingness to submit to the trial at hand? Has the question "Why me" become your first and last name? Do you feel that each experience of devastation has pushed you deeper into some dark, distant desert, leaving you feeling hidden in a valley of pain? If that sounds like you, then I have some good news for you.

You've been in search of your reason for surviving, but I want you to know that your reason for surviving has been looking for you too. God has a plan for your future, and He wants to draw you into your destiny.

Rebekah was one who was drawn to her destiny. God chose her as the wife of the patriarch Isaac, and He clearly had a plan and purpose for her. She was still a young woman when destiny called her, and the call would not leave her until she had agreed to move from the place she was then living. She had to step out, by faith, into the unknown, and thus, to step into the plan of purpose that was already set for her life.

When the story begins (in Genesis 24), Rebekah is not mentioned by name. This should give some of you hope today. You may not be hearing your name called right now, but God is having a conversation with destiny concerning you and your future at this very moment.

As Genesis 24 begins, Abraham, the father of faith, is giving his servant, Eliezer, an assignment. Essentially what he said to him was this: "I'm sending you as my trusted servant to find a suitable wife for my son Isaac. Here are my guidelines: First, don't look for a woman among the Canaanites. They refuse to reverence God, and they practice witchcraft, fornication, adultery, and many other ungodly things. Find a maiden worthy to be his bride from among those of my father's household."

Eliezer understood perfectly what was required of him and later repeated it word for word:

The Lord has blessed my master greatly, and he has become great; and He has given him flocks and herds, silver and gold, male and female servants, and camels and donkeys. And Sarah my master's wife bore a son to my master when she was old; and to him he has given all that he has. Now my master made me swear, saying, "You shall not take a wife for my son from the daughters of the Canaanites, in whose land I dwell; but you shall go to my father's house and to my kindred, and take a wife for my son."

Genesis 24:35-38, NKJ

Today, in the twenty-first century, we still have those who say that they're daughters in the house of God, and yet they don't live by or obey the rules of the Father. Nor do they respect the authority of His presence. Because of this, God is searching for a daughter who truly belongs to Him, one who is of the Father's house.

He's not interested in those who profess to be members of a church, or who have joined a service club or some other social organization. He's looking for daughters of His presence, those who have chosen to live a life of purity and holiness, a life that reflects His plan for their lives. These are the daughters of God who are about to experience an awesome visitation from Him. The destiny of favor to be found, or discovered, only rests on daughters who dwell in the Father's house.

This does not mean that we have to be perfect already in order to walk in our destiny. None of us is perfect yet. The only requirement is that we remain in the Father's house. He will do the rest.

3

Although Eliezer understood clearly his master's challenging command, he had one concern:

And I said to my master, "Perhaps the woman will not follow me."

Genesis 24:39, NKJ

It was a legitimate concern, but Abraham reassured his servant:

The Lord, before whom I walk, will send His angel with you and prosper your way; and you shall take a wife for my son from my family and from my father's house.

Genesis 24:40, NKJ

As these divine revelations unfold, know that someone's looking for you, and you're destined to be favored with discovery. God will even send angels to facilitate your entry into destiny and protect you until it comes to pass. This may sound totally absurd to you at the moment, for you may be feeling lost about now. If so, rest in the knowledge that you'll soon be found.

Faith to Believe

In this passage of scripture, Abraham represents God the Father, Isaac represents Jesus, God's Son, and Eliezer the servant represents the Holy Spirit, the anointing of God. Rebekah represents you. You're the sacred vessel that the anointing is looking for. You're destined to receive and hold what God has sent forth. Can you believe for it?

It takes faith to believe that you're the one whom God has been preparing to walk in such great destiny, to live a life that will bring glory to His name. You may not be able to see what God sees in you, and that's where faith comes in. You may not feel that you can do what He feels you can do. But if He said it, then believe it.

If God has said that this is what you were created to do, then simply accept that fact. There can be no debate with the Creator of the universe. He is truth, and what He says is always true. Your duty is to believe.

God is not asking you to understand His plans and purposes for your life; He's just asking you to accept His call. He'll do the rest.

God Is Tracking Your Every Move

Your mind may still be flooded with questions. For instance, "How will my destiny find me under the load of burdens and despair I carry?" Don't worry about it. The Creator placed a special tracking device in your heart before He sent you into this world. You've never been totally lost from Him. He's been monitoring your every move from a distance, and He knows right where to find you.

When the servant asked Abraham how he could convince the woman he was sent to find to make the journey back with him, Abraham basically said, "If you find a real daughter of God, one who has been pre-selected especially for this purpose, you won't have to convince her to come back with you. She'll come willingly."

Once you connect with the real reason you're here on this earth, it will bring a peace to your spirit that cannot be

5

explained. When destiny finds you, you'll breathe a sigh of relief, as the feeling of being lost leaves you and the feelings of being found rushes in to take its place. It's a totally transforming experience.

The Anointing Will Seek You Out

To me, one of the most powerful ingredients, or key revelations, in our gourmet spiritual dish called *Drawn to Destiny* is the beauty of the operation of God's anointing. It will never have to struggle with you. Because you're favored by God, it will find you, and once you're found, you will not struggle against your revealed destiny.

Relax in the arms of His anointing, embrace your destiny, and be carried along by its flow.

Stop worrying about how you'll get to where God is taking you. Relax in the arms of His anointing, embrace your destiny, and be carried along by its flow.

Abraham's search for a proper wife for Isaac demonstrates to us how you, as a real daughter of God, can accomplish your divine assignment, your true destiny in life. It doesn't depend on you, but on God's Spirit. You need only cooperate with His urgings and go with Him where He leads you.

When the Spirit of God is released to search you out, it will be done in the timing of the Father. His timing may not seem appropriate to you. When He finds you, you may feel that you're on the verge of a mental collapse. But if God releases His anointing to find you, that breakdown will be canceled, and you'll be moved toward your divine destiny.

Abraham told Eliezer not to worry. There was a divine plan in place for the procurement of a suitable wife for Isaac. And because it was part of a divine plan, it would work. How comforting this is to know!

What Exactly Is Destiny?

Before we go any further, let's examine for a moment this word *destiny*. The word *destiny* is not found at all in the King James Version of the Bible and only once in the New King James Version (see Lamentations 1:9). *Webster's Dictionary* defines *destiny* as "a state or condition appointed or predetermined." Your destiny is what predetermines the course of events that will come to your life.

Destiny also means "the course of events, considered as something arranged by a power greater than man." So your destiny doesn't depend on you; it's controlled by God. That's good, for only He knows what's best for your life.

The word *destiny* was derived from the word *destination*, which means "the place set for the end of a journey." So your destiny is the place you're going in God.

God has long held this destiny in His heart. He said:

For I know the thoughts that I think towards you, saith the Lord, thoughts of peace, and not of evil, to give you an expected end.

Jeremiah 29:11

That *"expected end"* is your destiny, and if you want to know something about it, ask the Creator. Your destiny originated in His loving heart.

7

It would be foolish to ask mere mortal men about such things. Only God knows what He's had in store for your life ever since you were nothing more than a passion in His heart. And now that you've become a manifestation of His mind's desire, there's no way that He'll allow you to go astray. He will see to it that you function as He designed you to function and that you accomplish what He created you to accomplish.

Those who try to live their lives according to their own plans most often end up in frustration. God has a plan for your life, an *"expected end,"* a destiny, and long ago He put that plan in place. That must mean that He expects you to make it to the end and not be short-circuited somewhere along the way.

Favored in This Fight

It seems popular today to tell people to seek after their own destiny, but that's not God's way. Since He's the author of our destiny, He has orchestrated every step of our life to pull us closer to our moment of favor. We were not designed to seek out our own destiny. Rather, destiny has been designed to seek us out.

At the precise moment when God's creative will faces His present timing in your life, your chosen destiny will collide with your present situation, and you'll be changed. When this happens, you'll immediately feel a warm embrace as a favored vessel under God's authority, and you'll know as never before that God has long ago set a divine plan in place for your life.

Another of the patriarchs, Joseph, gives us a clear understanding of what it means to be favored in the fight.

He received dreams of destiny concerning the plan of God for his life. When sharing this plan with his brothers (who didn't appreciate his dreams of destiny, nor the fact that he was excited to share the dreams with them), Joseph didn't yet understand that God's plan would take him on a long and lonely journey. But even though he would suffer many unpleasant things in the days ahead, Joseph, in the midst of his process of purpose, maintained the favor of God upon his life:

> *And Joseph's master took him, and put him into the prison, a place where the king's prisoners were bound: and he was there in the prison. But the Lord was with Joseph, and shewed him mercy, and gave him favour in the sight of the keeper of the prison.*
>
> *Genesis 39:20-21*

Even when Joseph was unjustly imprisoned, God was with him, and everything that he touched prospered.

You, too, may have been experiencing great adversities, as you have moved through your process of purpose, but the favor of God has never left you. Like Joseph, you may have found yourself sharing your purpose with others who could not appreciate the plan God had for your future (often because they were so focused on your past). But through it all, God's favor was still with you in the fight.

Take a moment now and look back over some of the situations that seemed to be the most difficult for you to go through. In doing so, you'll discover that you were anointed even then with the favor of God to prosper in a problematic situation.

9

You may find yourself completely surrounded by those who appear to be totally unaware that it's you whom God has sent His anointing to find. But get ready anyway. The plan is already in place, and your true purpose is about to be manifested.

In some cases, the last thing you may want to hear right now is what the apostle Paul wrote to the Church at Rome:

And we know that all things work together for good to them that love God, to them who are the called according to his purpose.

Romans 8:28

What did Paul mean by this? When God's timing of deliverance, success, or victory comes into your life, it doesn't matter what else is going on with you at that moment. God's timing will collide with trouble and manifest purpose. The favor of God has located you in the timing of God, and it's His plan and purpose that you now connect with your divine destiny in Him. So brace yourself for a collision!

Essential Spiritual Ingredients
Faith to relax with the favor to be found

Chapter Two

The Search

CAPEHART'S CORNER: *Allow the angels of anointing to prepare your spirit with the strength to stand!*

Angels in the Midst

Remember God's amazing promises to you from His Word. You've been set up as a real daughter of God. When God releases His anointing to come and find you, that anointing will not need to wrestle with your spirit. And the anointing sent forth from heaven will always find you, even if it takes an angel to clear the path for it.

In Genesis 24, the Lord essentially said to Eliezer, "I'm sending an angel to prosper you in your way." Imagine, when the anointing is coming your way, your angel is removing every hindrance that tries to stop God's anointing from

11

reaching you. Your angel will cast down every spirit of the enemy that tries to hinder you from reaching your destined place. The angel will also cast down every trap of the enemy set to keep you bound by the pressures of the past.

Too often, we think that the strongholds of the enemy, or what others do to hinder us, is the only thing that an angel is assigned to destroy. But I've found that the greatest strongholds, or hindrances, are the ones that we bring upon ourselves. They are strongholds of fear, doubt, intimidation, shame, guilt, low self esteem, etc. The angel God sends is not only commanded to deal with the devil; he's also commanded to deal with you. Although he will not wrestle with you, his assignment is to bring your spirit under subjection to the Lord.

Paul wrote to the Corinthian believers:

For the weapons of our warfare are not carnal, but mighty through God to the pulling down of strongholds; casting down imaginations and every high thing that exalteth itself against the knowledge of God, and bringing into captivity every thought to the obedience of Christ.

2 Corinthians 10:4-5

Open your Spirit and receive it. Everything that's trying to prevent your next breakthrough, everything that's trying to stop the next outpouring into your life will be blocked by God's angel, as he pulls down satanic strongholds and even your personal strongholds. Your angel is fighting to guarantee that you will receive all that God has for you. God has sent the anointing to find you, He has empowered His angels to fight for you, and it's all because He has chosen you to flourish.

12

Planted to Flourish

The righteous shall flourish like the palm tree: he shall grow like a cedar in Lebanon. Those that be planted in the house of the Lord shall flourish in the courts of our God.

Psalm 92:12-13

I recently heard someone say again, "It's time to bloom where you've been planted," and I began to understand what is meant by this statement. Most flowers are never given the choice of where they're to be planted. The only choice they have is to bloom or not to bloom where they happen to be planted.

Have you been planted? If so, have you decided to bloom? Or have you decided to be consumed? Will you allow the heat to destroy you? Or will you use the heat to fuel the growth process of your spirit? Will you complain about the constant battles with drought? Or will you learn to conserve every drop of rain to water your roots and eliminate pain?

Trust God and know that you're a woman who has been planted in the house of the Lord. As such, His anointing will always seek you out and find you. And why? So that you can flourish!

The meaning of this word *flourish* is "to prosper, to grow well." In Song of Solomon 7:7, the palm tree is a symbol of beauty and prosperity. God wants you to know that He has planted you in His house to flourish, and to that end, He will send divine favor upon your life.

Some time ago, after reading Psalm 92 again one day, I felt an intense need to understand what it meant to *"flourish like a palm tree ... in the courts of our God."* What I discovered

13

was that in biblical times every part of the palm tree was useful for something. The fruit of the palm provided food. The smaller leaves were used to make baskets, while the stronger leaves were used to make fences. Even the small threads in the leaves were woven together to make ropes. The juice of the palm tree was used to make a strong drink for medicinal purposes. And finally, the wood of the palm tree was used as building material or firewood.

After receiving this information, it seemed to me that the plan of God for the righteous in their development was simple. His desire is that you flourish like a palm tree, that is, that every part of your life be used to bring glory to His name. Your job, your family, your ministry, your mind, and your ambitions are all intended to bring glory to God. Every part of your life will be used, if you allow it to be used— even your weaknesses and your past failures.

The palm tree should symbolize your life prospering in every way, for there's nothing too small about your existence that God cannot use.

Strength to Stand

Another part of Psalm 92:12 says, *"He shall grow like a cedar in Lebanon."* The cedar tree is extremely long-lived, some being as old as one thousand years, and growing to a height of eighty to one hundred feet. The trunk of such trees can grow to forty feet in diameter. What a mighty tree!

In the life of the righteous, the cedar represents the strength that God will bestow upon you as you stand in your destiny being used by Him. In other words, you will be long-lasting in your life of destiny. You won't be, as many, a one-time wonder, but rather a wonder for life.

14

At one point, while I was preparing to minister on this passage of scripture, I was in the process of redecorating my home. I was so moved by the revelation I received from this psalm that I decorated the entire house in palm trees. I wanted each entry into my home to be a constant reminder that God was making my life to flourish and my spirit to prosper in every way.

He promised:

Beloved, I wish above all things that thou mayest prosper and be in health, even as thy soul prospereth.

3 John 2

I would like to encourage you to place a palm symbol somewhere in your surroundings so that it will be a constant reminder that God is about to cause you to flourish for His glory.

Planted in the House

Every one of us faces the challenge of wondering if we're in the right house, or the right ministry, and if we're doing the right assignment. Just being busy doesn't mean that you're doing the right thing. It's important to have clear directions from God concerning your life's assignment. He has a way of planting, or positioning, you in the right house, one where you can bloom and flourish in the area of your assignment.

Don't become confused if and when your house of destiny suddenly begins to look like a house of horrors. Trust and know that God is in control.

When you've been planted in an area by God for a specific reason, you may have to endure some trying moments.

These come in an attempt to uproot you from your position. You will surely go through tests and trials that will leave you questioning whether or not you're in the right place. If God has planted you in a certain position with a certain purpose, don't allow any trial to move you out of that position. God is in control, so relax and trust Him.

The psalmist declared:

And he shall be like a tree planted by the rivers of water, that bringeth forth his fruit in his season; his leaf also shall not wither; and whatsoever he doeth shall prosper.

Psalm 1:3

You may be experiencing a slow process of budding even though you know you're planted. If God has planted you, He will water you for growth. And if He has planted you, He'll cause the sun to shine on you (just as the rain falls on you). It's all part of the process of growth. And, if God has planted you, you can also know that whatever you do will prosper.

The prophet Jeremiah is an example of someone who was planted in the house of the Lord with a divine assignment, but that assignment was not easy to accomplish. He was assigned to warn the children of Israel to prepare and what the consequences would be if they failed to do it, but this assignment was met with great opposition from the very people he was sent to help. As a result, Jeremiah became very discouraged and wanted to quit. Instead, he found that he could not easily do it. He was planted in the house of God for a purpose. He said:

Then I said, I will not make mention of him, nor speak any more in his name. But his word was in mine heart as

16

a burning fire shut up in my bones, and I was weary with forbearing, and I could not stay. For I heard the defaming of many, fear on every side. Report, say they, and we will report it. All my familiars watched for my halting, saying, Peradventure he will be enticed, and we shall prevail against him, and we shall take our revenge on him. But the Lord is with me as a mighty terrible one: therefore my persecutors shall stumble, and they shall not prevail: they shall be greatly ashamed: for they shall not prosper; their everlasting confusion shall never be forgotten.

Jeremiah 20:9-11

Take these words of Jeremiah and use them to water your spirit during times of dryness due to temporary discouragement. Jeremiah declared that the Lord was with him as *"a mighty terrible one,"* and, therefore, the enemy would not prevail. This word is still true today. The enemy will not prevail—if you have been planted in the house of the Lord with purpose.

The enemy will not prevail—if you have been planted in the house of the Lord with purpose.

You will know that you've been planted in a particular ministry by God the moment you become angry, upset, discouraged, or despondent and declare that you're leaving, you're quitting, you're never going back ... only to realize that you can't quit. Even after you feel, or believe, that you simply cannot stand to bear another set-back, another heartbreak, another fall-out, or another pull-down, you somehow find yourself back in your rightful place with a praise of "yes" on your lips. You're singing, "I feel like going on. Though trials come on every hand, I feel like going on." Suddenly strength and courage seem to rise in your spirit, from some secret place of peace, and you continue to obey God. He, in turn, showers you again with the waters of worship and the light of His lifting power.

But what about the weeds that grow beside you in the garden? Although weeds in your planted place will attempt to choke the life out of your destiny, know that no weed can stop you from blooming. Don't worry about those who continue to attempt to hinder the assignment of God on your life through their constant taunts and mocking words. God is an anointed exterminator, and His weed-killing plan is powerful and effective. His Word declares:

Every plant, which my heavenly Father hath not planted, shall be rooted up.

Matthew 15:13

For the time being, you may have to allow some weeds to stand beside you in the garden, but know that they will soon be uprooted. They may be in the garden, but they're not part of the predetermined blooming.

"God's Anointing Is Not for Me"

Some might say, "But God's anointing is not for me." Yes it is! The Lord has led you to *Drawn to Destiny*, and He has done it for a purpose.

I can hear someone saying, "Dr. Capehart, I have much too much baggage and way too many problems, BIG problems, for God to be able to use me. I'm too far in debt, too far in sin, and too depressed to be of any use to anyone else." If that's you, I believe God is saying to you today, "I can work with you. All you need is My help."

Next, I hear Him commanding, "Angel, go relieve the pressure and the problems of My real daughter. Erase her past. Help her to start walking in My anointing. She is chosen and favored. My anointing is destined to find her and cause her to flourish." Please receive that as from the Lord to you personally today?

There's an angel working on your behalf. He's been appointed and equipped by God's power and authority to prepare the way for the anointing to prosper you. God's anointing will be able to get through to you because all the hindrances will be cleared away. By the time the anointing finds you, there will be nothing standing between you and the plan of God for your life. Every excuse, struggle, stronghold, and insecurity will be ultimately destroyed by the angel of the Lord sent to prepare a pathway for your destiny.

"But Dr. Capehart," someone might say, "you don't know what I've done and the company I've kept." That may be true, but the Lord isn't alarmed by where you came from; He's only interested in where you're going. The anointing cannot erase memories of abusive relationships, remove the pain of a bad marriage, or recapture the failed opportunities of your past, but your angel can uproot these hindrances and move them out of your way so that you can have a better tomorrow.

Prepare your heart to tell God "Yes" because you can no longer embrace the excuses of "No." They're no longer valid.

And now, I pray that those of you who have been wounded and left with scars from the past would allow the Gardener to replenish your spirit with the refreshing soil of hope. Allow the warmth of His touch to wash you clean, as He removes any broken pieces, which, if left unresolved, would not allow you to bloom as the beautiful flower He has created and planted you to be.

Essential Spiritual Ingredients
Peace to accept the assignment for your life and begin to bloom in the garden where God has planted you

Chapter Three

The Place of Promise

CAPEHART'S CORNER: *Be in the right place with God (in prayer, fasting, and worship) when destiny comes looking for you!*

*G*od's anointing found Rebekah at the well, the place that Abraham's servant, through prayer and worship, had decided would be the place of destiny. And destiny must find you in your prearranged place of purpose when it's time for you to come forth.

Eliezer prayed a simple, but powerful prayer that day:

O Lord God of my master Abraham, please give me success this day, and show kindness to my master Abraham.

Genesis 24:12, NKJ

God honored this humble prayer, and when Rebekah was drawn to the well and to him, Abraham's messenger was faithful to recognize the hand of God in the events that were unfolding. He began to worship God, thanking Him for His good favor toward his master Abraham:

> *Then the man bowed down his head and worshiped the Lord. And he said, "Blessed be the Lord God of my master Abraham, who has not forsaken His mercy and His truth toward my master. As for me, being on the way, the Lord led me to the house of my master's brethren."*
>
> *Genesis 24:26-27, NKJ*

In order for God to bless you on your road to destiny, you must position yourself somewhere along that road.

⚭

It's extremely important that you be in the right place with God when destiny comes looking for you. You cannot afford to miss your season of spring because you're going through a winter of worry. Always remember that seasons are just that—seasons. They will soon pass. The Scriptures teach us this truth:

> *To every thing there is a season, and a time to every purpose under the heaven.*
>
> *Ecclesiastes 3:1*

The servant (God's Spirit, His anointing) knew that it was Isaac's time in destiny to have a wife, and he was sent to find that destined wife. Therefore as he went on his way, he prayed that Isaac's predestined wife would be in her place. In order for God to bless you on your road to destiny, you must position yourself somewhere along that road.

Drawn to the Well

As I studied this passage, I asked God, "Lord, how was Rebekah drawn to the well? How was she drawn to her destiny?" The Lord lovingly reminded me that all of His daughters, at some point in their lives, ask Him this same question. All of His daughters need to be *Drawn to Destiny*.

Have you ever said anything like this to God?

"Lord, how did I get here? I wasn't supposed to be anointed."

"Lord, I wasn't supposed to make it this far in life. Can You tell me how I got here?"

"Lord, how did I survive all the adversity, the storms of my past? Somehow, someway, You brought me through the lies, the deception, and the 'mess'. Lord, how did that happen?"

If you've asked the Lord questions like these, you're not alone. Most of us have asked these same questions. And God understands why we ask them.

When I asked Him how Rebekah had been drawn to the well, He spoke the following words into my spirit:

Tell my real daughters that before they made it to this earth, before their own mothers knew them, I knew they wouldn't want to come to the well, their place of destiny. I couldn't trust them to come to the well on their own.

23

Before I sent them forth into a world full of tests and trials, I tied them to Me. I tied them with a promise of a chosen life that could never be broken by any situation, a promise that would bring glory to My name.

I knew they would get into some messy situations. I knew there would be times in their lives when they would not know they were anointed. I knew there would be days when they would not even know Me, days when they would stumble, and I would need to be there to catch them before they fell.

I knew there would be days when it looked like all hope was gone, their lives would seem useless, and the devil would tell them that they could not make it. I knew it would require a long process before they could find themselves at the well. I patiently waited as each dilemma drew them one step closer to their destined course."

And God's Sprit is drawing you too.

Don't Play Tug of War

Do you remember the old childhood game called "Tug of War"? It's a game in which two players get a rope, they mark the center of that rope, and then they retreat to each end of the rope and begin to pull. Each player pulls with all their might, trying to pull the other player onto their side.

Usually the match goes back and forth, as each player uses every ounce of available strength to keep the other player from pulling them across the center. The player who finally pulls the other to his side wins the game.

This might be a nice game, but, friend, God doesn't want to be constantly playing "Tug of War" with you. He's tired of trying to pull you to your destiny, while you're trying to pull Him into your desperate dilemma. Unlike in a game of "Tug of War," when we allow ourselves to be pulled to God's side, we don't lose. Everyone who is pulled to His side wins.

So stop struggling against Him. Just drop your end of the rope. Don't keep trying to pull God in your direction. It's a losing proposition. Relax, and let God pull you to His side.

Are we so foolish as to wrestle against God? His strength can outlast ours any day. You've jockeyed for position long enough. Now, it's time for the last pull. This time, He wants His pull to bring you to His side once and for all. The game is over, and, by allowing Him to win, you win too.

Your Struggle Is Over

God wants you to know who you are in Him. He would say to you today:

"My daughter, you're never alone. You may have been by yourself, but you were never alone. Even when you found Me, turned your back on Me, thought you got away, and then started walking away from Me, I wouldn't let you go. I still had a hold on your spirit.

"If I need to wait a year while you wrestle with a stronghold, I'll wait. Even when you entered into My presence and declared, 'Lord, this is my last time. I've finally left the world, and my desire for the world is over,' I knew your good intentions would not last. I

knew the moment you left My presence that you'd be back in the arms of the enemy.

"I had to let you walk through many flames of fire, but I never allowed you to be burned. I had to allow you to swim in deep waters, but I would never stand by and watch you drown. So I said, 'No matter what, she's Mine. I will never let her go. I'm snatching her out of the fire. I'm pulling her from deep waters. It's time for her struggle to be over.' "

Do you see it? The time of your struggle is over! The Lord is declaring:

"My real daughter, I have watched you long enough. I've waited long enough. The anointing is about to penetrate your spirit and draw you closer to Me, as you seek Me through prayer and worship."

Get ready. It's time for the anointing to turn everything that's been locked up and stored up, everything connected, everything appointed, everything chosen, into a place in His presence where His spirit literally overtakes you!

The Lord knows where you are, and He'll not let you fall. But your upcoming breakthroughs will always start with prayer and worship. He has said:

The steps of a good man [woman] are ordered by the Lord: and he delighteth in his [her] way. Though he [she] fall, he [she] shall not be utterly cast down: for the Lord upholdeth him [her] with his hand.

Psalm 37:23-24

The Place of Promise

Say this prayer out loud as you worship the Lord today:

Dear Lord, I know that as I walk through my trials, You'll always be there with me. I don't mind going through the fire, and I've tried my best to find the real fire.

Lord, by the time I complete this book, I pray that I will no longer need to worry because by the time I see the fire, I'll have already walked through it. By the time a situation hits, You will take the sting out of it.

Lord, thank You for ordering my steps.

Amen!

Essential Spiritual Ingredients
Prayer and worship

Chapter Four

The Worship at the Well

CAPEHART'S CORNER: *Nothing must hinder you from getting to the place of worship and praise when the timing of destiny begins to draw you in!*

Seasons of Worship

Many times, in a "dry season," you cannot feel the anointing that already resides within you. You pray, but it feels as though the Lord is not listening. You fast, yet nothing seems to happen. The more you fast and pray, the worse the drought seems to get. The more you worship, the worse you feel.

Your experience at the well did not happen because you prayed. You didn't get there because you fasted. You got there because you were drawn there by the timing of destiny on your life. Jesus said:

29

No man can come to me, except the Father which hath sent me draw him: and I will raise him up at the last day.

John 6:44

Friend, no matter what happens, stay near the well the Lord has drawn you to, and don't move until He tells you to. Trust God. He has something in store for you there, something that will revolutionize your life. Stay at the well and patiently wait, watch, worship, and pray.

No matter what well you're standing near right now, no matter what "mess," what trauma, what dilemma, what suffering and pain you're in, trust God and stand until you see His work. God knows and sees your struggles, He knows you're there at the well, and He will soon draw you to your destiny.

Although it may appear to others like you've lost your mind, although it may seem that your family is about to be separated, although it may seem that you're about to die with cancer, the Lord is right there with you, and His anointing is on its way. No matter what your current circumstances may be, go into prayer and worship. Boldly declare the truth of Psalm 28:7:

The Lord is my strength and my shield; my heart trusted in Him, and I am helped; therefore my heart greatly rejoiceth; and with my song will I praise him.

Psalm 28:7

When you declare to Him, "Lord, I love You," your mouth and heart become dedicated to Him. Have faith in Him, even when you don't know what you're doing at the well, and continue to worship Him.

My favorite time to worship is when I'm by myself. I like to pray alone because then I'm not inclined to worry about how I look, how I'm dressed, or what others are thinking about me. I don't have to act like I'm "all that." I can just simply say, "Father, I need You to help me."

If you're presently standing at a well, and don't know why you're there, trust God. Remember, He takes the things of the foolish and uses them to confound the wise:

But God hath chosen the foolish things of the world to confound the wise; and God hath chosen the weak things of the world to confound the things which are mighty.

1 Corinthians 1:27

You may be going through some things right now that you don't understand, but trust God. Others are saying, "I would not do that if I were you. That looks crazy." Trust God and keep on worshipping Him—no matter what the circumstances.

Hannah's Choice

You have a choice to make. Will you or will you not worship God in the midst of your circumstances?

Most of us know the story of Hannah. She lived with her husband, Elkanah, and his other wife, Peninnah. The problem was that Peninnah had borne Elkanah several children, but Hannah was barren. Peninnah taunted Hannah because of her barrenness

The matter reached a climax one day when Elkanah had taken the entire family for their annual appearance at the tabernacle in Shiloh (see 1 Samuel 1:1-8). Hannah suddenly knew that she had a choice to make. She could become bitter and lose God's blessing, or she could choose to worship Him and pray. Hannah chose the better part.

As Hannah was praying at Shiloh, she cried out with such passion that Eli, the High Priest at the time, saw her and thought that she had probably overindulged in wine and was drunk. When he looked closer and saw that she was sober and that she was praying with fervor, passion, and sincerity; he agreed with her for her petition for a son.

What kept Hannah in the presence of God despite the frustration of her barrenness and the taunts of Peninnah? I believe it was the same thing that keeps driving you and me back into His presence—purpose and destiny. Even though you don't yet see the manifestation of His promise, you must still thank Him. You must still trust Him and believe His Word—despite what a doctor might say and despite what the "evidence" might indicate.

There was something inside of Hannah that drove her to worship. She could have stayed home in discouragement and declared, "I pray, but nothing happens. I fast, but nothing happens. I intercede, but nothing happens." Instead, Hannah determined that she would thank God in spite of all the contrary evidence. She realized that it was her time to be blessed.

You've probably said something like this yourself: "God, I've been coming to You year after year. I've been trusting You for a very long time now. I've been waiting for my life to change." Well, if that's so, your time for change is finally here!

Hannah declared that this was her year, this was her time, and Eli was so impressed with her sincerity that he was moved to agree with her for her petition:

The Worship at the Well

Then Eli answered and said, "Go in peace, and the God of Israel grant your petition which you have asked of Him."

1 Samuel 1:17, NKJ

Make a decree for yourself today. Declare that this is your year, your time to receive your promised miracle. Let the Peninnahs in your life continue to laugh and taunt you publicly, if they will, but you must continue your private petitions of prayer. God always answers the persistent heart.

"Lord, Make Me Productive"

Hannah was tired of barrenness, and I trust that you're tired of it too. Many of us have probably said to God something like:

"Lord, I seem to have everything I need to get the job done, but nothing is happening."

"Lord, I have money and I have talent, but I'm still not producing."

"Lord, why is it that I still feel dead, even though Your Word says, 'I have given you life and life more abundantly'? Lord, instead of me producing life, I seem to be producing death."

Many people would have looked upon Hannah as a blessed woman and wondered why she was not satisfied with what she already had. Her man, Elkanah, loved her so much that he wanted to give her a double portion:

33

But to Hannah he would give a double portion, for he loved Hannah, although the Lord had closed her womb.

1 Samuel 1:5, NKJ

But there was a reason Hannah was not satisfied. I can somehow hear her praying, "God, I know You love me, but I'm tired of worshipping without producing the spirit of worship in the church." Let me explain what I mean by that.

When God has anointed you to birth something, you're not satisfied just to bring it to life for yourself. You want to bless others too. That's why Hannah made her vow to God:

Then she made a vow and said, "O Lord of hosts, if You will indeed look on the affliction of your maidservant and remember me, and not forget your maidservant, but will give your maidservant a male child, then I will give him to the Lord all the days of his life, and no razor shall come upon his head."

1 Samuel 1:11, NKJ

Hannah wanted to offer back to God what He was offering to her. When you start exercising the gifts God has given you and giving out to others, when you start bringing life into the dead situations of those around you, then you're fully functioning as one of God's real daughters.

Don't "Mess Up" While You're Shut Up

Hanna had a husband who loved her, and she had the physical tools to produce a baby, but, for some reason, she couldn't seem to get pregnant. The Bible is clear that God Himself was responsible for this: *"For the Lord had shut up her womb"* (1 Samuel 1:5). So, although she seemed to have everything she needed in place, she could not produce. She was barren.

Be careful how you go through your time of barrenness, don't allow yourself to become bitter because of the battle, and don't allow yourself to stop believing in God's promise just because of the strain of your struggle.

I believe that Hannah declared within herself, "I can't afford to 'mess up' while I'm shut up." No doubt she had heard about two other women of ancient times (both of them mentioned prominently in the book of Genesis) who had been in the very same situation and had not handled it well.

...although she seemed to have everything she needed in place, she could not produce.

There was Sarah, who had a promise to produce out of her barrenness, but who "messed up" while she was shut up, when she gave Hagar, her handmaid, to Abraham, to produce an heir. The result was Ishmael, but he was not the son God had promises.

Then there was Rachel, who was also barren. Caught in a similar situation, she gave Bilhah, her handmaiden, to Jacob and that union produced two sons, Dan and Naphtali. Later, this barren woman would give birth to two sons.

Hanna made up her mind not to settle for an imitation miracle. She wanted to produce her own miracle in the timing of God. She didn't want the promise without the pain necessary to produce it. Please, don't settle for a substitute miracle birthed by someone else. God has a personal miracle waiting for you.

Make a decision within yourself not to "mess up" while you're shut up. Don't take matters into your own hands in the hope of producing your promise sooner. If you do that, what comes out may be a monster rather than a miracle.

A New Prayer

It's good when we can pray, "God, I bless You for what You're doing in my life. Lord, they said I wasn't going to make it, but You helped me. Lord, I thank You that I'm no longer depressed. I thank You that I'm free in the name of Jesus." But, as good as that is, it's not enough to pray that kind of prayer and then come to church and sit quietly in a pew, thanking God for what He's done for you, while many of those around you are still dead and dried up and depressed. If you're not producing peace in the Church, God wants to give you a new prayer! Hannah was not satisfied, and her spiritual dissatisfaction caused her to pray a new kind of prayer.

By offering her yet-unborn son to the Lord, Hannah was saying, "Lord, it's not enough that You just bless me. Give me a son for Your glory, and use him to bless others. Use what you will allow me to produce to extend your Kingdom." That's a prayer that brings satisfaction.

Many of you who are reading this have more than enough possessions, more than enough money, more than enough clothes, and more than enough cars. Because of that, you know that life is more than physical things. Now, you want to produce spiritual things, the things of God.

Hannah said, "Lord, I know You've blessed me with material blessings while I was barren. I appreciate the herds

You've given me, the shelter You've given me, the husband You've given me. You gave me all of those things, but my womb has been dead. God, I'm not satisfied. This time, I will not settle for a blessing with a dead womb. Now I want to be blessed so that I can produce a blessing for others."

It's time for you, as a real daughter, to go beyond your own personal blessing and move to a point where you're a blessing to others. It's not acceptable to be blessed when your entire neighborhood needs to become sanctified. When Hannah entered into worship with her God, she asked Him to open her womb so that she could produce everything He created her to produce.

Peninnah may think that you're still barren, but she's not aware of what God has told you in private. Don't push her out of your life just yet. She has to hang around until you give birth. Even then, once you deliver, you should be courteous and send her a "thank you" card. Let her know that it was she who provoked you to your true purpose in life. Thank her for pushing you to pray so passionately.

As David sang:

Thou preparest a table before me in the presence of mine enemies.

Psalm 23:5

Thank God for the Peninnahs who provoke us!

"Valley Girls"

Don't spend too much time focusing on the taunts and threats of the Peninnahs around you. Be prepared to accept the fact that you'll have to go through a valley experience before you can handle the anointing of your destiny. And, very often, when you're going through your time of being formed, you'll encounter two types of people.

I have come to call these two types of people the "pullers" and the "pushers." "Pullers" will come and go in your life. Their main agenda is to pull you down, take you backwards, or, at the very least, to stop you from going forward. Don't be surprised when a "puller" suddenly withdraws from your life. They were only meant to stay around for a season.

But there are other individuals who will come into your life with an assignment from God to push you to your purpose. These are the "pushers," and you'll always need some of them in your life to push you to do what God has created you to do. People who are used by God to push you forward are of the utmost blessing to your life.

The "pushers" who have been assigned to your life will be with you through all of life's ups and downs. They'll support you when you succeed, and they'll encourage you when you're down. They'll be your strength when you're weak, and they'll correct you when you're wrong.

No matter what you go through, you can always count on the "pushers" to be your "valley girls." Valley girls are those sisters in your life who have seen you at your worst and still appreciate your best, sisters who were patient with you in the valley and are proud of you on the mountaintop. Everyone should maintain positive relationships with such women.

Valley girls will always rejoice with you when your time of destiny arrives, because they've seen the struggles you passed through to get there. Do you have any valley girls in your life? If not, ask God to give you some, and if so, appreciate the role of encouragement they play.

Get this into your spirit: you are loaded with purpose. God is about to stir you up and release destiny over your life. It's your time to be a blessing, to be used for His glory.

Like Hannah, let your problems provoke you to passionately pray for your destiny. Develop a genuine hunger and thirst for the purpose of the Lord to come forth in your life. Jesus said, *"Blessed are they which do hunger and thirst after righteousness: for they shall be filled"* (Matthew 5:6).

Essential Spiritual Ingredients
A passion for your purpose

Part Two

The Preparation

Chapter Five

The Making of a Great Name

CAPEHART'S CORNER: *If you know who you are in God and you walk in your divine inheritance, you're destined to receive a daughter's blessings from your Father's house! So move forward, divinely directed!*

"Whose Daughter Art Thou"?

As a daughter of God, it's important for you to know and understand who you are in Him. When you know your divine heritage, then your expectations are focused on eternal matters, and nothing in this material world can interfere with God's plan for your life.

When Rebekah visited the well to draw water, she was asked the question that all of us must answer, *"Whose daughter art thou?"* It makes no difference if you're a housewife, a physical therapist, a conference speaker, or the president of a multi-million-dollar corporation. Unless you know the answer to that simple, yet profound, question, your life will meander meaninglessly.

> *And [Eliezer] said, Whose daughter art thou? tell me, I pray thee: is there room in thy father's house for us to lodge in? And she said unto him, I am the daughter of Bethuel the son of Milcah, which she bare unto Nahor.*
>
> *Genesis 24:23-24*

Rebekah knew and clearly understood her heritage, her lineage, and she proudly responded with her father's name, Bethuel. Bethuel means "separated unto God." By answering in this way, Rebekah was reaffirming the fact that she was birthed out of a heritage that was separated from the beginning for the glory of God.

And in the very beginning of your life, God separated you for Himself as well. This is why you don't fit into the plan of the enemy.

But if you were asked that same question today, how would you answer? I pray that you would say, "I am a daughter from the house of my Father!" No matter where you are today, you must be assured in your heart that you were birthed out of a divine heritage to bring glory to God.

You may have once been part of a lineage of rejection and shame, but, thank God, you were found and adopted and given full benefits as a real daughter in the house of your heavenly Father.

44

It's Not the Devil

God wants you to know that what you've been going through has nothing to do with the devil. It has to do with you not understanding who you are in Him, not understanding your spiritual heritage.

When we're tested and tried, God sometimes exposes our sins to the world so that He can force us to recognize, once again, who we are in Him. That's why everyone suddenly knows that you're about to go bankrupt because you've mismanaged your finances. That's why you suddenly lost your job for deceptive practices you thought no one else even noticed. That's

...your problems have nothing to do with the devil. It's you God wants to deal with.

why your adultery has suddenly been exposed—even though you were oh so careful to conceal it.

And it was oh so stupid of you to try to somehow justify it. "How can it be wrong when it feels so right?" you wondered aloud. Foolish daughter!

If you think you know who you are in Christ, if you claim to be a daughter of the Father, then when was the last time you had a family meeting with God to discuss your life, your sins, your behavior, your attitude, and your problems? When you're chosen by God, you're corrected for change, not ignored and tolerated. You see, your problems have nothing to do with the devil. It's you God wants to deal with.

When God challenged me to write *Drawn to Destiny*, He wanted me to tell you that you're His daughter, a daughter of destiny, and that your time of exposure (public embarrassment) and trial is about to come to an end! Father has called you in for a meeting.

A Name for His Glory

The great wise Solomon declared:

A good name is rather to be chosen that great riches, and loving favour rather than silver and gold.

Proverbs 22:1

As impossible as it seems, God is about to bring you to a place in Him where even your name will honor Him. God told Abraham:

And I will make of thee a great nation, and I will bless thee, and make thy name great; and thou shalt be a blessing.

Genesis 12:2

Not only is God drawing you to your destiny for fulfill-ment of who you are in Him, but He's also drawing you to your destiny so that your name can declare in the earth who He is. This section is for those whose name has been mired in messy situations, who have been called in the past such names as liar, cheater, fornicator—or worse. But today you're on a journey, being drawn from the depths of destruction and despair to the doors of divine destiny.

It's not God's desire to make your name great (through godly character and integrity and great accomplishments) so that someone may worship or adore you. He will make your name great in Him so that your accomplishments will cause others to worship Him. Therefore, He is seeking those who simply want Him to use them to set the captives free. Not all of those running to Him and calling out, "Use me! Anoint me! Let me preach!" will be heard. This may not be for them, because when the fire gets hot, they jump up and run.

God is seeking those who stand in holiness before Him by what they're doing and have done, as opposed to what they say. He is more impressed when your character mirrors His image rather than when you just talk about Him.

I've often heard saints say, "I'm too saved now to do this or that." For instance, "If someone slaps me, I'll turn the other cheek." They only say that because no one has slapped them yet. You'll never know what you've truly been delivered from until you've been tested in that area. The Lord is raising up people in this hour who will do more than talk. They will defy all odds and overcome the devil.

Obey His Voice

There are too many people talking about having had a name change, but their character remains the same. They're still speaking the same old things out of their mouths. Their feet are still going in the same old paths. That's why the world has a problem with what they say.

Abraham had to learn obedience to God:

Now the Lord had said unto Abram, Get thee out of thy country, and from thy kindred, and from thy father's house, unto a land that I will shew thee: And I will make of thee a great nation, and I will bless thee, and make thy name great; and thou shalt be a blessing: And I will bless them that bless thee, and curse him that curseth thee: and in thee shall all families of the earth be blessed.

Genesis 12:1-3

What brings glory to God? You bring glory to God when you fulfill the assignment placed upon your life. Many of us walk around all our lives not even knowing our purpose. We're quick to assist others in finding their purpose, but we seem to fall short when it's our turn.

God spoke to Abram and told him to get up from where he was, to leave his country and his family, and to go to a land that He would show him. He wouldn't let Abram see anything until he first got up.

We often ask God to show us this or show us that. We feel that we need more clarification. But when God spoke to Abram and told him to leave, Abram knew immediately what he had to do. He had heard the voice of God.

In order to obey God, you must first believe that what you have heard was from His voice calling you to your destiny. If you do not believe that, you'll never move an inch.

Secondly, you must then obey the voice you've heard. Many people say that they've heard the Lord speak to them, but they never move forward. They never obey what the voice of the Lord has commanded.

When we hear the voice, then it's time to obey. It's not enough to say, "I'll go when I have the money." God didn't tell Abram to go when he received the money. He just said, "Go." He didn't tell Abram to go when he felt like he had sufficient knowledge. He just said, "Go."

Even if you don't feel worthy, if God said, "Go," then He expects you to go. You may be hurting when you hear His voice, but you can go hurting and be healed in the way. You may be broken when you hear His voice, but you can go broken and be made whole as you go. You may be going through something terrible when you hear His voice, but you can go while you're still going through that thing, and find ease in the way.

You may be afraid, but that doesn't change God's command. Do what He says—even if you're afraid, and He'll take away every fear. Whatever your situation happens to be, that doesn't change anything. Just do what the Lord has spoken to you to do, and He will do the rest.

Thirdly, you must be totally led by the voice of the Lord, through faith. You may not, and probably will not, understand where you're going, but you'll go because you walk by faith and not by sight. And as you walk by faith, the Lord will anoint your hands and your feet to fulfill your assignment.

Destiny Is Not Lost, So Don't Get Off Track

You must trust God to lead you and guide you, because you're headed to a destined place. It's not a hidden place, and you're not lost to it. It's simply a matter of knowing which way to take. Just follow His directions.

We often make our assignments difficult because of the way we've been taught to walk in them. The Lord is looking for people who not only know how to pray, but also know how to get up off of their knees and walk out the directions they've received through prayer.

And what happens if you get off the course God sets for you? Does that change your destiny? No, all you have to do is get back on course. Your destiny doesn't change because you happened to get off track.

God is looking for someone to walk the destined path so that glory can be brought to His name. He said, *"I know the thoughts that I think toward you."* In this context, the word *think* indicates that He keeps you on His mind. When you understand that, you're constantly on God's mind and in His Spirit, your walk and destiny will become more real to you.

You must make a conscious decision to fulfill your destiny, and that requires obedience. Telling others about your destiny is not enough. They'll not believe you until you've stepped out and are actually walking in it. The enemy will refuse to believe you until you yourself refuse to doubt.

The Making of a Great Name

How will your name become great in God? He will make it great.

This word *make* means "to develop with only the necessary ingredients." The Lord will only use the things in your life that He needs to make your name great. Everything else will be eliminated.

God told Abram to go away from his family, and there are some things in your life right now that God has already told you to let go of. There are some people in your life who cannot go with you into your destiny.

Lot started out with Abram, but God would not show Abram his full destiny until he and Lot had separated. God told Abram, "Look where you are now" (see Genesis 13:14).

Some of you are already in the place of your destiny, but you can't see it for the distractions around you.

Your place of destiny is not always where you think it is. It may be in the complete opposite direction of where you are now. And sometimes God will show you things only after you've separated yourself from things He has told you to get away from.

Your place of destiny is not always where you think it is.

Why did He give this promise to *"make"* Abram's *"name great"*? I believe it's because there are too many believers walking around blessed, but their names are still "a mess." Their name still shows up in lies and gossip. God wants to make our name great to glorify His name, but, for far too many, their reputation doesn't match their anointing.

God began to take Abram on a journey to develop his life. He had to change his name to match the depth of his destiny. So God changed it from Abram, which means "exalted father," to Abraham, "the father of multitudes." God also changed the name of Abraham's wife. She had been Sarai, which meant "princess," but now she was Sarah, which means "the mother of princesses."

You must allow God to develop your character over time to match the depth of your destiny. You can't have a great destiny with a shabby reputation and a name of shame. Many of us will never get to our destiny because we don't want to be made great.

We know that we were created in God's image. This word *create* means "to bring into existence." But we also need to be made by God. *Made* means "to reconstruct

51

something or rebuild it; to bring about; to prepare; to dress for a part; to cause to be." So why do we have to be made after we're already created? When God created you, He created you in His heart and in His spirit. He first created you in the heavens, but now He must make you in the earth so that everyone can see that you were created in His image.

God has to make you, or rebuild you, so that He can burn out everything in your spirit that's not of Him. He has to eliminate all of the contaminated elements that have somehow attached themselves to your purpose. Some of us become so torn down in life that God has to rebuild us in love. It's time for an overhaul so that God can then make our names great.

Is What I Heard True?

When people hear your name, they should think of the Lord's image connected to your name. But many of us don't carry ourselves like we believe that. Many saints jeopardize the name of God by their ungodly and careless acts.

There's the constant mishandling of finances, which leads some to a lifestyle of check bouncing? When this happens, what kind of name are we declaring in the financial institutions of our community? What are we saying to the people who work there about how our God leads us to conduct business? It is important that our name, in any given situation, should only be tied to holiness and righteousness.

Solomon's name brought glory to God:

And when the queen of Sheba heard of the fame of Solomon concerning the name of the Lord, she came to prove him with hard questions. And Solomon told her all her questions:

there was not any thing hid from the king, which he told her not. And when the queen of Sheba had seen all Solomon's wisdom, and the house that he had built, And the meat of his table, and the sitting of his servants, and the attendance of his ministers, and their apparel, and his cupbearers, and his ascent by which he went up unto the house of the Lord; there was no more spirit in her. And she said to the king, It was a true report that I heard in mine own land of thy acts and of thy wisdom.

1 King 10:1 and 3-6

The Queen of Sheba was not disappointed when she met Solomon. He fully lived up to his reputation. Prepare yourself for others to challenge the purity of your name in God, and do not be found lacking.

The only way for the people of the world to see Christ is for them to see Him through His children. Jesus said:

Let your light so shine before men, that they may see your good works, and glorify your Father which is in heaven.

Matthew 5:16

When people hear your name, that very name, through a lifestyle of integrity and godly character, should instantly cause others to want to serve your God. When that is true, you shall then begin to walk in the fourth promise of Abraham. You will go from being blessed to being a blessing. How wonderful it will be when God blesses you with a new home, and you, in turn, can buy someone else a new home. God is trying to teach us how to be more than just blessed; He's trying to teach us to be a blessing. Learn to be led by His Spirit so that the blessings of His favor upon your life can make your name great, and you can then begin to bless the lives of others.

Your Name Identifies Who You Are

He that overcometh, the same shall be clothed in white raiment; and I will not blot out his name out of the book of life, but I will confess his name before my Father, and before his angels.

Revelation 3:5

Can you imagine it? On that great day in the heavenlies, Jesus will look at you, and then turn to the Father and say, "Father, You remember *[here He will insert your name]*. Well, she made it in. She had some ups and downs. She had some problems that no one thought she could overcome, but she made it."

Next, the Scriptures tell us, after Jesus has confessed your name to the Father, He will then go and tell the angels the good news that you've made it in. "They said she wouldn't make it," He will share. "They were sure that she wouldn't be here today. But, thank God, she's here." What a wonderful day of rejoicing that will be!

Essential Spiritual Ingredients
The courage to choose godly character to reflect His image through the power of a great name

Chapter Six

The Meeting at the Altar

Capehart's Corner: *When you come out of God's presence this time, the enemy will see His glory on your
face! You won't need to tell him where you've been!
He'll know!*

Build Seven Altars

One day, as I was praying, the Lord spoke to me and
said, "If you want to flow in My power to perform,
take a closer look in My Word at what Balaam did." I read
the story again:

*And he [Balaam] said unto Balak, Stand here by thy
burnt offering, while I meet the LORD yonder.*

Numbers 23:15

55

The Lord asked me, "My Daughter, what is an altar?"

"Lord, it's a place of sacrifice and a place of worship," I respectfully answered.

"That's right," He said. You see, when the enemy began to talk to Balaam and to try to confuse him, attempting to convince him to curse what God had blessed, Balaam came back with a word of his own. He said, "Balak, build me seven altars."

Imagine that! Balaam ordered his enemy to build him seven places of worship. Balaam essentially said, "Don't just build me one. Build me seven altars." In other words, "By the time I get through worshipping at all of these altars, whatever the Lord says will be settled, and the enemy's plan will be done away with through God's power to perform." Amazingly, the enemy built the seven places of worship for Balaam.

Instead of complaining about what's going wrong in your life—the bad finances and the constant family struggles, build an altar to your Lord and Savior and start to praise Him for every circumstance in your life. Praise is a key dimension God uses to flow His power to perform and transform into your life.

When your heart is right and when God sees that He can trust you, then He releases His power to perform through you, saying, "Okay, she's about ready for My next blessing, for My next transformation in her life."

Leave Your Problems at the Altar

After Balak built the seven altars, Balaam offered up his sacrifice to God. Then he said a very interesting thing to Balak: "Now you stay here at the altar while I go meet the Lord."

The Meeting at the Altar

Can you imagine that? Once the enemy builds you a place of worship, leave him at the altar while you go meet with the Lord. Balaam essentially commanded his enemy to stay there at the altar while he went to meet with God.

As you're reading *Drawn to Destiny*, I believe that God would say to you today:

> *Bring all of your problems to the altar and leave them there. Then, come up to a higher place to meet Me. You don't need to stay there struggling with your troubles.*

While you're there at the altar, tell the enemy to "stay there" while you go and meet with the Lord. Make it clear what you want him to do. He is to stay behind while you advance into God's presence.

At this point, I asked God, "Lord, why did Balaam need to leave the enemy there and go up higher?" The Lord revealed to me that it wasn't so much the act of bringing the enemy to the altar that was significant, but that we bring the lie to the altar. Whatever the enemy has said about you that is a lie, place that lie on the altar, since a lie cannot remain in the presence of the Lord.

Maybe you'll come to the altar with the lie that your marriage is about over. Don't worry. God says that your marriage will be transformed. So, leave that lie on the altar, and come up higher—up where the presence of the Lord dwells.

Meet With Him, But Remain Quiet

And the Lord met Balaam, and put a word in his mouth, and said, Go again unto Balak, and say thus.

Numbers 23:16

The Lord met Balaam, put a simple and critical word into his mouth, and told him, *"Go again."* Daughter of God, here's your simple revelation: You're about to go again. The last time you stepped out in Jesus' name, you may have failed the test, but now you're about to go again. Things may look bad, but go again to the altar, and watch how Jesus will resolve your crisis.

This time, you're going to the altar with more of His power and more of His authority. This time, you've met with God, and He has put a word in your mouth. His life-changing Word says, in essence: "My daughter, you can do it!"

The enemy will not give up so easily:

And when he came to him, behold, he stood by his burnt offering, and the princes of Moab with him. And Balak said unto him, What hath the Lord spoken?

Numbers 23:17

It may seem strange to some that Balaam didn't answer his enemy, but when you come out of worship and out of the presence of the Lord, after meeting Him at the altar, you don't have to announce it. You don't have to tell the devil: "I've been in the throne room of the Most High God, and now I've got a burning word in my belly. You cannot touch the anointing that's upon me. And I'm coming after you." In fact, you won't have to say a word.

When you come out of God's presence this time, the enemy will see the Father's glory on your face. So, you won't need to tell him where you've been. He'll know it just by the way you look and by your manner.

Of course, the devil is forever curious about how to bring you down, so he'll probably still ask you, *"What hath the Lord spoken?"*

And, yes, you do know what the Lord has spoken to you, but you don't need to share that revelation with the enemy in words. You only need to answer through your faith and your faith-filled actions.

How does this revelation apply in practice to your daily life? Some of you reading *Drawn to Destiny* will return back after prayer to your situations that have been pressing you down, expecting to verbally hurl scriptures in the atmosphere and scream rebukes at the enemy in order to calm the raging seas of your life. Instead of saying a word to the areas of need in your life, just stand back and watch the walls of confusion quickly fall, as the proof of God's power is evident through the presence of His glory on your face.

So, go after a real encounter with God, one that goes beyond soft music, and the surface display of emotions. Rather, seek an encounter with God, in which His presence leaves you speechless.

His Word Cannot Be Reversed

And he took up his parable, and said, Rise up, Balak, and hear; hearken unto me, thou son of Zippor: God is not a man, that he should lie; neither the son of man, that he should repent: hath he said, and shall he not do it? or hath he spoken, and shall he not make it good? Behold, I have received commandment to bless: and he hath blessed; and I cannot reverse it.

Numbers 23:18-20

When God declares a promise over your life, that promise cannot be reversed. In other words, the enemy cannot change the promises of God or turn them around.

No matter what area of your life the enemy points to as proof of his victory or proof that your life is failing, reject his lies.

God's Word will never return to Him void. When the promises of hope that God sends out for your life return back to Him, the word can only come back to Him when it has fulfilled its assignment, that which it was sent to accomplish.

The Lord has declared that His Word and His promises that He has spoken over your life will come to fruition. He doesn't care what the enemy has said or tried to get you to believe. No matter what area of your life the enemy points to as proof of his victory or proof that your life is failing, reject his lies.

Put it all on the altar. Remember, God has picked you up and washed you in the blood of the Lamb. If He spoke it, and His Word cannot be reversed, then it is so.

If He spoke it, you're healed. If He has declared it, you're the head and not the tail. So, start saying to the enemy, "I know it looks like I'm going down, but I've received a revelation from the Lord. God is about to release in me a new thing, and it cannot be reversed. If God said it, that settles it. I can now shout for victory. Yes, I still have some issues to deal with, but God has already spoken to me about them."

Today, the Lord is speaking to you and reminding you of His promises:

"What did I declare to you during the meeting at the altar? What did I tell you I would do for you? And what did I say I would do through you? If I showed that to you, then I'm able to give you My transforming power to perform it. If I spoke it, I shall yet do it. Even though you need to wait until your appointed date has fully come, please know that I'm coming to give you My power to perform."

Do you see it? When God speaks it, His Word is set, and the things He speaks are placed into non-retrievable motion. Once He declares a thing, He releases it, and then it's on its way into your life. He cannot and He will not call it back. His words cannot be reversed. So, whatever the Lord has spoken is in the process of happening. Once it's on, it's on, and nothing can change it.

Going Beyond What Can Be Measured

And Balak said unto Balaam, Neither curse them at all, nor bless them at all.

Numbers 23:25

When you were a youngster growing up, someone may have said to you, "I'm going to beat you up after school." If so, that declaration was based on the fact that you looked to them like a chump. But what that person may not have known was that, on your way to the playground, you went past the spiritual phone booth. (For anyone who doesn't understand this, I'll get to an explanation shortly.) When that person picked a fight with you, they saw what they could see, but they didn't know you had a source of power that their eyes could not possibly behold and their senses could not possibly measure. In this way, you learned very early in life that others should not judge you by what they saw. You have known for years in the pit of your belly that if you opened your mouth and spoke one word, God would back you up. "I will honor what My daughter declares," He affirms.

If you speak to a mountain, then that mountain has to move (see Matthew 17:20). If you bind a spirit here on earth, that same spirit is bound in heaven (see Matthew 16:19). If you loose prosperity into your life here on earth, God will loose that prosperity in heaven.

Don't you dare let others prejudge you by what they see. There's so much more to you than the outer appearance.

Repeat God's Word

But Balaam answered and said unto Balak, Told not I thee, saying ... ?

Numbers 23:26

With this, Balaam repeated himself. He essentially said, "You must not have heard me the first time I spoke to you concerning this situation. Let me tell you again."

Jesus used this same spiritual tactic:

And he cometh to Bethsaida; and they bring a blind man unto him, and besought him to touch him. And he took the blind man by the hand, and led him out of the town; and when he had spit on his eyes, and put his hands upon him, he asked him if he saw ought. And he looked up, and said, I see men as trees, walking. After that he put his hands again upon his eyes, and made him look up: and he was restored, and saw every man clearly.

Mark 8:22-24

When Jesus first prayed for the healing of a blind man, the result was that the man's vision was only partially restored. He could see men, but they looked like trees walking around. Jesus proceeded to pray for him again, and this time the man's vision was totally restored.

There may be times in your life when God has to touch you in your place of weakness more than once. I'm certainly not saying that the power of God is incapable of doing the job upon the first touch. I'm saying that God will continue to touch you until your issues become clear. In the same way, sometimes you must re-state the thing you have said before, not because you didn't believe it the first time, but because the devil is acting like he didn't hear you the first time.

I'm the blessed mother of two boys, who, at the time of this writing, are ages sixteen and thirteen. When I call out to my boys and say, "Brandon, Britton, come here," I'm confident that they've heard me. But my call doesn't always have the desired affect.

Brandon and Britton are active boys, and sometimes they continue to do what they've been doing before I called them. The second time I call them, I do it with much more emphasis. "Boys, I know you heard me the first time, but I need to let you know: this is the very last time I'm calling you." That gets their attention every time.

When you repeat something, it doesn't mean that you didn't believe it the first time around. You're just letting the enemy know that God means business; He's not playing around.

When you come out to face the devil, never run from him. He's the one who should run when he sees you having God's power to perform. Because of the way some Christians act, the devil believes that we're all wimps. On his next visit to you, I dare you to find a spiritual phone booth. In biblical terms, find yourself a prayer closet.

As children we learned about Superman. In the newsroom of the Daily Planet, a major metropolitan newspaper, the people around him knew him as Clark Kent, mild-mannered reporter. No doubt some even tried to push him around. "You don't have anything," they declared defiantly in his presence. Those who were trying to push him around were men with big muscles and small minds.

The executives of the newspaper may also have felt that they were superior to the lowly reporter. But then one day Clark Kent discovered that he had supernatural strength, and with that strength he could perform feats that others could only dream of doing. Every time he went into that phone booth, something started to happen.

While he was in the phone booth, he may have been saying to himself, "What in the world am I doing here? What is this anyway?" But he, and everyone else, would soon see what he had.

Your Spiritual Phone Booth

Sometimes you don't know your power until you get into the phone booth. For spiritual purposes, the phone booth is the presence of God, the secret place of prayer. When you're in His presence, He begins transforming your words and transforming your actions, until you stand up strong and firm and say, "The Lord is positively on my side. Whom shall I fear?"

When that happens, you begin to talk like you've never talked before, and you begin to walk like you've never walked before. Instead of walking with your head hung down, you now walk with your head up high and your chest out. And you begin to say things like, "Oh yes, I can do that, because the Lord said I can do it."

What was it that Balaam said to Balak?

Told not I thee, saying, All that the Lord speaketh, that I must do?

Numbers 23:26

Notice Balaam's language here. He didn't say, "All that the Lord speaks, I might do," or even "All that the Lord speaks, I will do." His words were much more emphatic, much more urgent. "All that the Lord speaks, I MUST do."

You're the vessel God wants to use in these final hours of spiritual history. You're the daughter of God who *must* go to the altar, and there you must leave all the lies, the deceptions, and every other hindrance. You're the one to whom God will give His power to perform, His power to transform both your life and the lives of others, as you seek Him out in a higher place.

You're the one God has pre-ordained to be drawn to your destiny.

Essential Spiritual Ingredients
*Willingness to stay in God's presence until
His glory is revealed in your life*

Chapter Seven

The Restoration of the Righteous

CAPEHART'S CORNER: *God will always chasten those whom He loves! Once the discipline process is over, He still considers you a chosen vessel, even if you're in need of restoration!*

We're All Miriams

Miriam, the older sister of Moses, has much to teach us about divine destiny. As a prophetess who led the women of Israel in worship, she was fully and abundantly walking in her own divine destiny. At the crossing of the Red Sea, for instance, responding to the song of victory led by

Moses, she encouraged the other women to sing, joyfully play their tambourines, and dance before the Lord:

And Miriam the prophetess, the sister of Aaron, took a timbrel in her hand; and all the women went out after her with timbrels and with dances. And Miriam answered them, Sing ye to the Lord, for he hath triumphed gloriously; the horse and his rider hath he thrown into the sea.

Exodus 15:20-21

At this point in her life, Miriam clearly could answer the question, "Whose daughter art thou?" And, because she knew who she was in the Lord, she was a force to be reckoned with.

It wasn't Moses, or Aaron, or any of the other priests who picked up a tambourine and began to sing in that moment. It was Miriam. And when Miriam picked up her tambourine and began to sing praises to God, *"all"* of the women followed her lead.

Clearly, Miriam had a positive relationship with the women in her camp, and she must have presented an awesome image as their leader. I honestly don't know many women today who could have done what she did that day. To get *"all,"* an absolute majority of the women present in the camp, to follow her was phenomenal.

In today's world, if I'm leading a conference, and I call for a time of praise and worship, I may get a majority of the women present to join me. I might even get the response of ninety percent of the women there. But there are always some who insist on standing off to one side and saying, "Not me! I'm not doing that. Banging on that old tambourine looks stupid. Dr. Capehart should just stick to preaching." How phenomenal that Miriam got the response of *"all"*!

But later in life, there was some strife in the camp, and Miriam joined others in murmuring against Moses (see Numbers 12:1-15). God was not pleased with this, and He asked His daughter, Miriam:

> *Wherefore then were ye not afraid to speak against my servant Moses?*
>
> *Numbers 12:8*

Despite the fact that Miriam was a greatly respected prophetess in her own right, one who had a large following, because God loved her, and because she was His daughter, He needed to discipline her at this point. In effect, He said to her, "Okay now, Missy, you're getting out of line here. It's time for Me to show you something about your divine heritage."

God had every right to be angry with Miriam. Because of who she was, she was required to live by a higher standard of conduct. This was unacceptable, and therefore He released upon her a unique type of punishment, one that would bring her public embarrassment, as well as the feeling of total alienation from her position in God:

> *And the cloud departed from off the tabernacle; and behold, Miriam became leprous, white as snow: and Aaron looked upon Miriam, and, behold, she was leprous.*
>
> *Numbers 12:10*

Fortunately for Miriam, her leprosy was not a permanent affliction. It lasted for only seven days, but that was long enough to impress upon her the importance of her divine destiny and heritage.

Are You In a Seven-Day Trial?

Is Miriam's staggering experience ringing true in your life as well today? Frankly, we're all Miriams, and we can all expect to experience His loving rebuke. How many times have you felt the power of God in your life, felt *Drawn to Destiny*, only to discover that you had suddenly and unexpectedly fallen out of His favor. It may not have been for murmuring, but for some other sin. Suddenly, you were white with spiritual leprosy, and you didn't know why.

Miriam suffered this terrible affliction for seven days. If you will allow me some creative license here, I believe that those days went something like our own periods of trial frequently go.

On the first day, she probably thought, "I can't believe this is happening to me. Lord, I'm Your faithful daughter. I'm the praise and worship leader. I sing songs that usher in Your presence. I'm a tithe-payer."

On the second day, she probably thought, "Oh my, everyone knows what I'm going through. How embarrassing! Lord, couldn't You have thought of something else other than leprosy to use to punish me? Give me a quiet storm and a secret struggle to endure, but, please, not a public display of destruction!"

On the third day, she was probably ready to cry out, "Lord Jesus, just help me. I'm getting Your point, and this is not fun!"

The Restoration of the Righteous

On the fourth day, she no doubt felt deep frustration, and declared, "Lord, I can't believe I'm still out here. I know You said 'seven days,' but I thought You really meant seven hours. I thought I would be released early from my punishment due to good behavior."

On the fifth day, she probably said, "Hey, God, I've been out here too long now. My time of punishment should be over by this time. I feel abandoned and alone. Have You forgotten me?"

On the sixth day, she must have thought, "Lord, please let me be healed. Enough is enough."

But remember, the Lord had said seven days, and He's a God who cannot lie. She would have to bear her humiliation for seven full days.

As that final, seventh day, approached, I believe Miriam stopped her crying and began to shout for joy because she knew that her road of sorrow was almost over. She knew that it would end after one week because her Father had spoken it.

It was nearly over now, and she was overcome with joy because the experience she thought, at times, would bring her death had become, instead, a testimony of surviving in the hands of the Father during a time of rebuke.

Our loving Father declared:

As many as I love, I rebuke and chasten: be zealous therefore, and repent.

Revelation 3:19

After seven days of being white with leprosy, Miriam was once again reminded of that vital question we must all

71

answer: *"Whose daughter art thou?"* Now, she knew more than ever what the answer was.

Pick Up Your Tambourine and Shout!

Have you been going through your own personal seven days of trial as God's daughter? Have you been going through a public embarrassment, or humiliation, in front of your family, friends, and neighbors that you don't understand? Daughter of God, are you ready to dare to shout to the Lord in joy because your time of leprosy is nearing an end? I believe God now wants to say to you:

"You're My precious daughter, and dear one, your seven days of trial are almost over!"

So pick up your tambourine and begin to shout!

Your Destiny Is Already Birthed

When Moses was a baby and was placed in a small ark in the river Nile to save his life, who was it who was assigned to watch over him and see that no harm came to him? Who was it that facilitated the events that would ultimately determine the destiny, not only of Moses, but also of the children of Israel as a whole? It was, of course, this same Miriam:

And his sister stood afar off, to wit what would be done to him. And the daughter of Pharaoh came down to wash herself at the river; and her maidens walked along by the river's side; and when she saw the ark among the flags, she sent her maid to fetch it. And when she had opened it, she saw the child: and, behold, the babe wept. And she had

72

compassion on him, and said, This is one of the Hebrews' children. Then said his sister to Pharaoh's daughter, Shall I go and call to thee a nurse of the Hebrew women, that she may nurse the child for thee? And Pharaoh's daughter said to her, Go. And the maid went and called the child's mother.

Exodus 2:4-8

When the mother of Moses put him into the river to hide him from the enemy, it was Miriam who was placed near-by to watch and to make sure her baby brother would be safe. She was still there watching when Pharaoh's daughter found Moses floating on the current.

When you're God's daughter, and you know it,

When you're God's daughter, and you know it, He'll use you powerfully to help unfold His divine plan. That plan has been predes-tined. It was set in place even when you yourself were but a babe. Still, sometimes God is forced to temporarily place seven days of leprosy upon your life, but He has a purpose in doing it. It will keep you on track, bring you closer to Him, and keep you subject to the leading of His Holy Spirit.

It was Miriam's idea to say to the Pharaoh's daughter that day, "Hey, do you need a nurse for that kid? I can go get you someone." When the princess agreed, Miriam then ran home and declared, "Mama, I know where little baby brother Moses is, and he needs a nurse! Come on, Mama, you're still going to be able to raise Moses to be a man of God."

With that foundation, let us move forward and look at what Miriam's baby brother thought and said when God struck his sister with leprosy:

73

And Moses cried unto the Lord, saying, Heal her now, O God, I beseech thee. And the Lord said unto Moses, If her father had but spit in her face, should she not be ashamed seven days? let her be shut out from the camp seven days, and after that let her be received in again.

Numbers 12:13-14

Moses cried out to God on Miriam's behalf because he remembered hearing about that time in his own life when, if it had not been for Miriam, there may not have been a Moses leading the children of Israel. Moses essentially told God, "Lord, I can't stand to see the sister I love suffer. Oh, I know she may have talked about me behind my back, but that's not important at the moment. It's what she did for me when I was floating on the river that matters most."

Yes, there have been times in your life when God led you to do things on His behalf, things that were desperately needed by the Body of Christ. Like Miriam, you served your Father well when He challenged you to a specific task. God knows your glorious past. But He also knows that your present struggles and problems will serve the purpose of bringing you into your future destiny.

Outside the Gate

Even if you're currently *"shut out from the camp"* for seven days, even if you're still standing outside the gate waiting to be let back in, God wants you to know that He sees His daughter, and He's supernaturally drawing you to your destiny.

God would say to you today:

74

"Yes, I know you've messed up. And I know you've been in pain during this period of your life. I know you're standing at the gate and feel like you'll never enter in again. But, My daughter, now's your time to be healed, and soon the gates will be flung open wide, and you will be once again welcomed inside."

God heard Miriam speak out against Moses, so He was forced to demonstrate His justice. But He also had not forgotten Miriam's destiny. He had called her and her two brothers, Aaron and Moses, for service and had commissioned each one of them, in their own way, to walk out their destiny among His people. Yet, all three of them stumbled at some point—just as you and I do.

Moses, called by God to minister to his people, became frustrated because the people he was called to lead so frequently challenged his leadership. This caused him to question whether or not he was hearing from God. When even Miriam (and Aaron) murmured against him, Moses must have uttered something like, "Lord, help me. What's going on here? Even my older sister and my trusted brother, my best friends in the whole world, are murmuring against me."

Miriam was called to be God's daughter, and she was anointed and appointed, yet she became angry and spoke against the leadership of her brother. When this happened, God basically said to her, "My daughter, be careful when things you don't like are happening around you. Be careful when you think I'm not moving fast enough for your comfort."

Aaron was also guilty of murmuring on this occasion, but, amazingly, he was acquitted by God's grace. As Miriam went through her suffering, he knew that she was suffering for the same thing he had done, and he was humbled by the fact that God had spared him from a well-earned punishment. That Miriam suffered and Aaron didn't is not easy to understand. Leave all such matters in the hands of the Righteous Judge.

Don't Touch God's Anointed

Why was God so severe with Miriam? Personally, I believe that it was because she was so anointed in her own right, and yet she dared to use her anointing against His anointing. God was telling Miriam to be careful how she used her anointing.

When our anointing is used against others whom God also anoints, then we're put outside the gates of the city for a period of time. Why Aaron escaped the same fate we can only wonder.

Many of you who are reading this book may have been put out of the camp for seven days. But God would have you know that you're still part of His Body. You've been temporarily put out of His presence because He wants you to understand the power you have in your tongue. He wants you to understand the power of the anointing that rests upon you, as His chosen daughter, and He wants you to remain receptive to the leading of the Holy Spirit as He continues to draw you to your destiny.

Until You Come Back

Because of your call, because you're chosen, because you're His daughter, He will bring you back. Be patient.

76

The Restoration of the Righteous

Notice the response of the other children of Israel to Miriam being shut outside the city:

And Miriam was shut out from the camp seven days: and the people journeyed not till Miriam was brought in again.

Numbers 12:15

The body, as a whole, could not move on until Miriam had been restored back to them. To me, this is one of the most powerful demonstrations of God's love for us. Even though Miriam had "messed up" and had to be rebuked and even put out of the city, everyone else was placed on hold until her time of rebuke had ended.

It's time that we, as the Body of Christ, realized that we're all needed in order to fulfill the call of God in the Kingdom. Though some may feel that Miriam should have been permanently excommunicated, God wants us to realize the importance of the anointing that was upon her life. God not only let her back in to show His love for her; He let her back in because she was important to the others.

Right now, there are a multitude of Miriams standing at the gate of the Church, and they're about to be received back in. As these "shut-out ones" enter in, a flood of God's power will come with them. So, get ready for the greatest move of God in our time.

Whatever you do, don't leave Miriam outside the gate. You cannot go forth until she has been fully restored.

Is Miriam Your Problem?

We're all Miriams, we all have problems in our lives, and, as we said at the beginning of this chapter, we can all

77

learn from Miriam's experiences. When it happens, don't insist on rehashing what sent you to the gate in the first place, and don't let it send you back out of God's presence again. Get victory over that thing. If you've had a problem with your tongue, put it under the control of the Holy Spirit now so that you and others can move forward.

If you have a husband or an outcast son or daughter who is currently standing at the gate of your life for their sin, when their time of exile is over, please let them come back into the family fold. At this very moment, the Church at large is at a standstill, and the Body of Christ is in the seventh day. What has been exiled and is even now at the gate is about to return.

As God's daughter, your time of trial is over. Whatever you've been going through, that time is ended. Where there has been a drought, it's now time for God's abundant rain. Because you know the answer to the question, *"Whose daughter art thou?"*, it's now your time to move on to your destiny.

Don't let any temporary setback stop you from fulfilling God's plan for your life. Even if you're standing outside of the gates right now, remember that you're still His daughter, and He has a mighty plan for your life. That plan includes reentry into the city—in His proper timing:

For his anger endureth but a moment; in his favour is life: weeping may endure for a night, but joy cometh in the morning.

Psalm 30:5

Essential Spiritual Ingredients

Patience to persevere in the midst of loving discipline

Chapter Eight

The Daily Turn

CAPEHART'S CORNER: *You're connected to God's Spirit, and He's guiding you through every obstacle in life to draw you ever closer to Himself!*

Don't Be Embarrassed to Start Over

When you understand that life is all about learning from your experiences and even from your mistakes, you'll find it easier to start over again after any setback. Start by admitting that whatever you're doing or did is not working. Admitting that something's not working is not the same as calling it a total failure. It's simply saying that it's time to reexamine all of the issues and try another approach. The destination remains the same, but the tactic will change.

Many find this process to be very difficult. Too often, precious time is spent trying to resurrect something that was never designed to survive in the first place. Admit that it's time to move on, and then move on. The greatest challenge in life is the ability to know when change is needed:

The word which came to Jeremiah from the Lord, saying, Arise, and go down to the potter's house, and there I will cause thee to hear my words. … And behold, he wrought a work on the wheels. And the vessel that he made of clay was marred in the hand of the potter: so he made it again another vessel, as seemed good to the potter to make it.

Then the word of the Lord came to me, saying, O house of Israel, cannot I do with you as this potter? saith the Lord. Behold, as the clay is in the potter's hand, so are ye in mine hand, O house of Israel.

Jeremiah 18:1-6

It is the Potter who knows what He has in mind when He creates a specific vessel, and when it does not come out as He wishes, He sets about to remake it. First, He crushes it, and it becomes nothing more than a lump of clay.

This crushing, however, does not signify doom or destruction; this crushing signifies "deliverance and destiny." As the Potter places you back on the wheel to develop your spirit to walk in your destiny, prepare yourself to make a daily turn.

Prepare Yourself to Make a Daily Turn

Monday: Prepare a Plan through the Power of Prayer

Make this a day of prayer and ask God, "Why am I here?" Begin to develop a plan, a purpose through prayer, and then walk according to the plan that God reveals to you in prayer.

Be sensitive to the voice of God during your prayer time. Listen for His voice as He gives you instructions on the next move for your life. These instructions may come through prayer or through the reading of His Word. Remember that your steps can only be ordered by the Lord if you remain sensitive to His voice and follow His instructions.

Tuesday: Develop the Courage to Change Completely with the Counsel of Correction

Have the courage to allow correction to bring you closer to the level that God wants for you. Godly correction may come through the reading of the Word, directly from the Spirit of the Lord, or from a message given by those in authority over you. It may well come to you through your spiritual mothers and fathers.

Don't quickly judge the words of correction from those in authority over you to be mere criticism. Use this as a time to grow. Remember that God chastens those whom He loves (see Hebrews 12:6).

The psalmist declared:

Thou shalt guide me with thy counsel, and afterward receive me to glory.

Psalm 73:24

Wednesday: Steps Ordered in the Season of God through the Strength of Salvation

Knowing when to move and when to stand still is imperative in your walk to destiny. Your clock may seem to be ticking faster than God's, but His clock will always have the correct time. While you're waiting on instructions from Him, use your time of waiting as an opportunity to make sure that your soul is anchored in the Lord, so that you can stand strong in your season of appointed assignment. Use this time to purify yourself through fasting and consecration. Focusing on future goals without preparing for tomorrow's instructions is a sure plan for failure.

Begin to pull down every stronghold that is placed to hinder you from reaching your destiny.

Thursday: Become Determined to Destroy all Doubts and Thoughts of Defeat through Deliverance

Begin to pull down every stronghold that is placed to hinder you from reaching your destiny. It's not the comments of others that tend to slow you down; it's the still, small voice pounding inside of you as a constant reminder that you're not equipped to do what you're trying to do in the Kingdom of God. Take your doubts to Him in prayer.

Friday: Adopt the Mind to Expect the Manifestation of Miracles

You must begin to develop the mind of Christ and expect miracles to happen on a daily basis. Miracles, for a believer, should not be considered as some strange thing. Many believers don't see frequent manifestations of miracles simply because they don't believe for them. Saying that you believe with your mouth is not the same as believing with your mind. You must first believe in your mind. Receive the mind of Christ, and know that He has promised:

All things are possible to him that believeth.

Mark 9:23

Saturday: Accept the Anointing to Achieve in All Areas with Assurance

Don't be afraid to walk in the anointing to achieve everything that God has laid out for you in His plan. Achieving is not a sign of arrogance; it's a sign of assurance in the anointing. It's God's desire for you to reach your destiny that was set for you before the foundation of the world. Be determined to achieve in all areas of your life, not just in the areas that are observed by others. Be committed to achieve even in your most private areas, when only you and God know.

Cleanse thou me from secret faults.

Psalm 19:12

Sunday: The Wisdom to Wait on God in the Atmosphere of Worship

Worship is an experience that brings about closeness to the Lord. Worship prepares your ears to hear His voice. It equips your spirit to obey His instructions. It prepares your heart to handle the journey toward destiny. It eliminates elements in your soul that can hinder your moment of breakthrough. Waiting in the presence of God through worship gives you the wisdom to walk through life with God as your Eternal Guide.

But as for me, I will come into thy house in the multitude of thy mercy: and in thy fear will I worship toward thy holy temple.

Psalm 5:7

After reviewing this seven-day turn on the Potter's wheel, I suggest that you start each day with a word of prayer focused on one specific area of growth. During these prayer times, always be honest with yourself and with God. Ask the Lord to guide you in each area, as you continue to walk toward your destiny.

Essential Spiritual Ingredients
Stability to handle the constant turns of change that are necessary to prepare you for your purpose

Chapter Nine

The Moment of
Manifestation

CAPEHART'S CORNER: *You can be in God's plan, living where He wants you to live and doing what He want you to do, and still experience times of testing, trial, and barrenness!*

A Moment with God

Have you ever encountered a situation that knocked you off your feet, simply because it caught you totally by surprise? Did it take you some time to gather yourself before you were able to respond to what happened? Did the shock of it leave you speechless?

Chances are you've been through a situation like this at some point in your life. If not, keep living, and you will. It's during times like this that a clear response is usually given, "I'll be all right if you can just give me a moment."

One day I found myself making this very statement, after having just received some bad news from my doctor. He said there were some abnormal test results from a recent examination I'd undergone. This caught me totally by surprise, and for some few seconds, I was left speechless. For those who know me, I know that may be hard to believe. But it's true.

The doctor asked if I was going to be all right, and, of course, I responded, "Yes, just give me a moment."

What does it really mean to need a moment to catch our breath and to digest what we've just heard? In the gospel of Mark there's a powerful illustration of a woman who simply needed a moment. She was desperate, for time was running out for her.

This was the woman with the issue of blood, a woman who had been struggling with her situation for twelve long years before she heard about Jesus. When she did hear about Him, she decided that she must make her way to Him. Her approach was firmly established: *"If I may but touch his garment, I shall be whole"* (Matthew 9:21). It's all right to have a desire and know what you want the Lord to do before you enter His presence. Knowing your need can hurry your answer.

The woman's story unfolds in this way:

And behold, there cometh one of the rulers of the synagogue, Jairus by name; and when he saw him [Jesus], he fell at his feet, And besought him greatly, saying, My little daughter lieth at the point of death: I pray thee, come and lay thy hands on her, that she may be healed; and she shall live. And Jesus went with him; and much people followed him, and thronged him.

And a certain woman, which had an issue of blood twelve years, And had suffered many things of many physicians, and had spent all that she had, and was nothing bettered, but rather grew worse, When she had heard of Jesus, came in the press behind, and touched his garment. For she said, If I may touch but his clothes, I shall be whole. And straightway the fountain of her blood was dried up; and she felt in her body that she was healed of that plague.

And Jesus, immediately knowing in himself that virtue had gone out of him, turned him about in the press, and said, Who touched my clothes?

And his disciples said unto him, Thou seest the multitude thronging thee, and sayest thou, Who touched me?

Mark 5:22-31

Help Me, Jesus!

A ruler named Jairus came to Jesus and passionately asked for help for his little daughter, who was at the point of death. He fell down at Jesus' feet and begged Him to come to his house. Jesus was so touched by this that He agreed to immediately go with the man.

While Jesus and Jairus were on their way to the home where the sick child was, people began to press toward Jesus from all sides. They were in front of Him, behind Him, and to the left and right of Him. Suddenly, *"a certain woman"* approached Jesus. The Scriptures do not reveal her name (perhaps intentionally), nor do they say where she came from. She was just *"a certain woman."*

I looked up the word *certain* in the dictionary, and one of the meanings of it is "destined." So it was a "destined woman" who touched Jesus that day.

People may not always call you by your name, but know that you are *"a certain woman,"* ordained to be *Drawn to Destiny* as a daughter of God. When God calls you *"a certain woman,"* it's because you're a destined woman, chosen by Him for His own purposes.

Upon her arrival in the presence of Jesus, this woman discovered that He was on His way to meet a twelve-year-old girl who was also in need of a miracle. She, quite possibly, would need a resurrection. No doubt, in her mind, the woman was saying, "If I could only have a moment with Him."

This word *moment* means "an instant or a very brief time." Sometimes you have to become so hungry for your healing and deliverance that you begin to believe that God can do it for you in a matter of a moment.

Jairus had gone to Jesus and asked Him to come to his house, and Jesus had agreed. Still, this woman was so desperate from suffering with an issue of blood for twelve years that she decided to risk interrupting their journey by approaching Jesus.

Why was this woman so bold? Because she had been consumed by this physical trial for twelve years already, and she'd made up her mind that enough was enough. For twelve years, she had grappled constantly with this matter. For twelve years, she had sought various doctors' advice, but nothing had helped. For twelve years, she had exhausted her finances, trying to find a solution, and it was all to no avail. Instead of getting better, she had only grown worse.

Can you imagine the short-lived joy and excitement she must have experienced after each encounter with what she thought would be her deliverance? And I'm sure that this has happened to you too. For you, it may have been while you were listening to a wonderful worship song. It was bringing you deliverance. But then, when you turned the tape off, you found that the problem had gotten worse, instead of better.

This had happened too many times, and the woman had now made up her mind. She was losing so much blood that something had to change, or she would soon die. She could not afford another imitation of hope; she needed a real break-through. So, when she heard about Jesus and His actions, she made up her mind to get to Him and touch Him.

The word on the street was that when Jesus showed up, He came in power, sovereignty, and with the ability to heal and set captives free. She needed that so desperately.

Daughter of God, if you're being subjected to a continuous trial right now, I pray that by the time you complete this chapter you'll be able to say, "I will not give up my destiny. I will touch Jesus and be healed once and for all."

This was a determined woman. She had been tried and tested for twelve years, and yet she was still declaring her hope: *"If I may touch but his clothes, I shall be whole."* But that would not be easy.

When Jairus had approached Jesus, he fell down on his knees, as he expressed his need. "I have a twelve-year-old daughter at home at the point of death." Jesus had been on His way to address that urgent need, and now a crowd had gathered around Him and was pressing Him with other needs. Still, this *"certain woman"* approached Him, not even caring if Jesus recognized her or not. She so desperately wanted her deliverance.

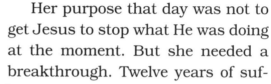

We want to "keep faking it" until we "make it."

Her purpose that day was not to get Jesus to stop what He was doing at the moment. But she needed a breakthrough. Twelve years of suffering was too much for any one person. She essentially said to herself, "I need His help, and I need it now. I honestly don't care who knows about my need and what they might think of how I intend to have it met."

Stop Faking It

This *"certain woman"* was like many of us. We want to "keep faking it" until we "make it." We like to act like we have it all together, but this woman didn't care who saw her or what they thought. She was willing to crawl on her knees, if necessary. In fact, she was willing to do whatever it took, to get to Jesus. Can you say the same today?

Can you declare, "Whatever it takes, I will get to Him. I may lose a few friends in the process, I may be lied about and talked about, and I may be judged unkindly for my worship because I'm so loud, but I don't care. Whatever it takes to get to Jesus, I'm going to do it"?

This *"certain woman"* had a made-up mind. She was going to get to Jesus, and nothing and no one was going to stop her. But before she could have made up her mind to go and find Jesus, she first had to hear about Him and know where He was. Somebody had to bring her this good news.

Thankfully, there are still people in the Church today who are sharing the Good News of Jesus. There are people who passionately love Him, and, people, and they want to see men and women saved, delivered, and healed.

Have You Recently Heard Good News?

Let me ask you an important question. Has anybody told you anything good lately? You might know some folks right now who are declaring desperation. You may even be one of them yourself. If so you'll surely recognize what they're saying, things like:

"I'm sick of this life."

"I'm tired of folks saying, 'He's a good God.' He hasn't been very good to me."

"I'm so frustrated that sometimes I feel like I just can't go on. And sometimes I don't even want to go on. Is life really worth living?"

If that's you, you have two choices: (1) You can decide to dwell on the negatives of life, and give up, or (2) You can do as this *"certain woman"* did and passionately seek Jesus.

When she heard the Good News, this lady with the issue of blood must have boldly declared, "Tell me all about Jesus," and when she had heard more, she judged it all to be true. She believed in Jesus, and that's what salvation is all about.

After her decision to believe in Him, she then made up her mind to go from where she was to where she wanted to be (where He was). Make up your mind today, no matter how painful it may be, to go from where you are now to where God wants you to be. The alternative is death.

Are You Bleeding to Death?

For some of you who are reading this book, whatever you've been doing is not working. Like that *"certain woman,"* you've already exhausted all of the conventional means of help, and you're still getting worse. You tried shouting it out. You tried praising it out. You tried crying it out. But none of those things seem to be working for you. Some of you have gone through some veritable spiritual conniptions in recent years (casting out demons, undergoing deliverances, and breaking generational curses), and still your situation remains the same. You're still "tied, tried, and tested" by your problems, with no apparent change in sight.

You have a spiritual issue of blood, yet you would be deeply embarrassed if anyone knew it. You have serious problems on the inside, but you try and camouflage them by wearing a new dress, adorning yourself in nice jewelry, sporting a modern hairstyle, and applying perfect makeup. But all of the camouflage won't cover up the truth. Maybe nobody knows it, but you're bleeding and in need of help.

I'm convinced that the reason so many of us miss what God wants to say to us from this passage about the *"certain woman"* is that we mistakenly believe that everybody knew about her and her problem. That was simply not the case.

94

The Moment of Manifestation

An issue of blood is something very personal. You could be standing next to *"a certain woman"* in a supermarket and never know that she had such a serious problem. You could be singing alongside her in the church choir or preaching with her at some national conference, and still you might not know that she was bleeding to death.

This *"certain woman"* could be a sister standing right next to you looking all holy and proper at the Sunday morning church service. You would never know. Or, this *"certain woman"* could be you.

To receive healing for something as serious as this issue of blood, a woman must first make the decision in her mind and then declare openly, "I'm sick of bleeding to death and sitting here faking it. I'm tired of acting like I've got it all together. I'm ready to risk being embarrassed by someone knowing the intimate details of my life. I simply have to get up from where I am and walk to where I can find Jesus."

When you're willing to risk all that you have with your decision, when you no longer care who knows about your condition, and as you passionately seek the hem of His garment, your bleeding will cease. Daughter of God, you've tried counseling, you've tried the best seminars, you've faithfully attended the most popular revivals in your city, and yet blood continues to flow from you. This is serious. It's time to stop trying to fake it, and just make your way to Jesus.

"Lord, Wash Me"

Some who are reading this book even now have kept their spiritual need inside for years. You've been able to successfully hide it from other people, but no more. It's time for everyone to see your real situation. It's time to admit that you've been faking your joy and laughter. It's time for you to admit, "I'm not nearly as healed or nearly as holy as you thought I was. I don't have the peace I've been claiming to have. Something on the inside of me is all 'messed up,' but I refuse to be embarrassed about it any longer. I need deliverance and healing, and I need it now."

Make up your mind to confront your spiritual issues, no matter who knows about it or what they may think. If someone tries to hinder you, you must declare, "I'm on my way to see the Lord, so get out of my way!"

Start crying out to the Lord, "Lord, wash me again. Clean me up, Jesus. Mold me again. I've got some 'stuff' on the inside of me that isn't holy. I want to be healed, and I could care less what other people think about my condition. I need You to wash me again, to create in me a clean heart, to purify my spirit and make me whole."

To be healed, after you've gotten up from where you are and after you've made up your mind, you must do something about your condition. If you don't, you'll die. You may not be in danger of physical death, but a spiritual one is even more serious. The next revival may be too late for you. The next prayer line might not help you. The next prophet may not call your name and pick you out of the crowd. You need to get to Jesus in a hurry.

Push Past Your Obstacles

Get with Jesus right now! Push past any other people that stand in your way, and push past any obstacles. Just get there, and you'll be made whole.

The *"certain woman"* heard about Jesus and believed that what she heard was true. Next, she made up her mind to get to Him. Then, she started on her way to find Him, determined to somehow enter His presence.

Jairus had gotten on his knees before Jesus because he had a daughter who was dying, and he, too, had made his way past every obstacle because of his deep need. If Jesus didn't show up at his house, his little girl would die.

It's not enough to just "hang around" where Jesus is and then say, "Yeah, I've been with Him." It's not enough to enjoy a reputation in your church of knowing Him. You must be willing to press through whatever stands in your way and actually get close to Him.

This requires a sincere urgency. You must cry:

"If I don't get to Jesus today, my household will perish."

"If I don't get to Jesus today, my debts will suffocate me."

"If I don't make it to Jesus today, I'll die from this terrible illness."

Go Ahead and Interrupt

Here's an incredible reality. This *"certain woman"* was faced with a dilemma: "Do I stop Jesus on His way to Jairus' home to heal his little girl, or do I timidly wait my turn in this long line?" I'm convinced that this woman was intelligent and cultured, but, at the same time, she was desperate. Within a matter of seconds, she had made her decision: "Jairus' daughter is not here, and I am here. Jesus has agreed to take the trip to see her, but I'm already here where He is at this moment. And I won't keep Him long. I wouldn't want Him to delay His journey to her, but I simply must touch Him for my own need."

The "certain woman" knew something wonderful: that she would only need to interrupt Jesus for one divine moment. That was all it would take. If she could just get that briefest of moments, all of her twelve years of personal misery would be over. Thus, the woman took her moment for a miracle, while passionately wanting not to hinder Jesus from fulfilling His assignment to answer the call of others. What an awesome woman she was!

Can you declare today, "Lord, I don't want to hinder You from helping others. All I need is to be in Your presence for a moment." Just a moment is all He needs to lift your heavy burden. Just a moment in His presence can ease your troubled mind. A moment in His arms can calm your raging sea. A moment with Him can bring you complete victory.

My Own Victory

After leaving the doctor's office that day, my first response was to call my husband. I longed to be held in his arms and reassured, but it would take me some time to get to him. I needed something quicker than that. I needed a moment to be held by the Lord.

As soon as I got in my car, I went for it. I took my moment with the Lord, and in that moment, He reassured me that everything would be fine. And it was fine! In the end, everything turned out just as He had said.

So, go ahead; take a moment in God's presence. Reach out and touch Him today in a way you've never experienced before. Daughter of God, it's time for you to passionately seek after Him, so that He can draw you closer to Himself. The Lord can touch you in an instant. So, take a moment, and let Him do it now.

It's time to turn our periods of intense trial into a permanent hope. In the very beginning, God declared your destiny. But even then He knew it would take years (perhaps as long as twelve or more) for you to submit to His plan for your life. To insure that you would make it to your predestined end, He connected you to His Spirit to guide you through every possible obstacle (of success, as well as failure). And, in this way, He has used every situation of your life to pull you closer to Himself. He created you to be *Drawn to Destiny*.

Essential Spiritual Ingredients
The boldness to break through barriers, believing for what lies beyond the battle

Part Three

The Sending Forth

Chapter Ten

The Release of the Righteous

CAPEHART'S CORNER: *Don't count your family and loved ones out! Their words of support and acceptance will come with the timing of your release!*

Returning to Genesis 24, let's take a look at how the final stages of destiny unfolded in the life of Rebekah and see her as she's finally standing in the face of destiny.

Eliezer placed beautiful rings on Rebekah's ears and bracelets on her wrists. This was not only a sign to *her* that she was God's chosen; it was also signified to *others* that she had been chosen by the Almighty:

And the servant brought forth jewels of silver, and jewels of gold, and raiment, and gave them to Rebekah: he gave

103

also to her brother and to her mother precious things.

Genesis 24:53

Rebekah was the chosen one, but Eliezer recognized that she must first be released by her family so that she could flow in her destiny. So he went to convince them to let her go, "Rebekah's the one God has chosen for the next dimension in Him," he must have said. "Will you now kindly release her to flow in His plan?"

Rebekah didn't have to ask her family to support her in her destiny; the anointing impressed their hearts to release her. In the same way, always remember that you'll never have to persuade others to support you in your purpose. The power of the anointing will impress upon them the need to release you to flow in your divine destiny, and this release will come in God's timing.

The earrings in this story represent the glory of God on your glowing face. The beautiful bracelets represent the mighty power of God that He is even now placing upon your hands. When God's glory has been placed upon you, and others see it, then it's time for you to go forth.

Your Family Will Be Blessed by Your Destiny

And her brother and her mother said, Let the damsel abide with us a few days, at the least ten; after that she shall go.

Genesis 24:55

Not surprisingly, Rebekah's family was at first reluctant to let her go, at least so quickly. Eliezer persisted, telling them that the Lord had prospered his way by leading him to Rebekah, a woman blessed beyond our common use of the word and that they would be wise to release her (see verse 56). Even when the initial reaction of others is "No," the anointing will always reveal to your loved ones that the necessity of your release is tied to their blessing and breakthrough.

When Eliezer gave precious jewelry to Rebekah and her family, he was demonstrating that because Rebekah was chosen by God and because she had been snatched out of the fire, not only would she be blessed, but they would be blessed as well. This encouraged them to release her.

So be careful who you're hindering, and be very careful not to leave too early when others are hindering you. The angel of the Lord will always make a way for you to be released to flow in the proper timing of God.

If others are laughing and making fun of you (perhaps even counting you out, expecting your past failures to be the fate of your future), it's only because they can't see your divine connection with God. They don't know that you're tied to Him and that one day He'll snatch you up and find a way to release you to flow into your destiny. Your connection may be an invisible cord that only you are aware of. You're aware of it because of the constant tugs felt in your spirit, as the Lord draws you closer to Himself.

Ten—Released to Flow

Eliezer replied to the request of Rebekah's family for a ten-day delay in her departure by saying:

Hinder me not, seeing the Lord hath prospered my way; send me away that I may go to my master.

Genesis 24:56

Of course, the family wanted to keep Rebekah close to them, and, of course, that's why they asked Eliezer to allow her to stay longer (at least ten more days). But what did the number ten signify in this case? I knew what the number ten meant biblically in most circumstances, but in the context of this story, I wasn't at all sure what the Lord was trying to say by it. When I asked Him, He seemed to show me that ten, in this context, meant "released to flow."

Please remember: delay does not mean denial.

This number ten first appeared in the story when Rebekah volunteered to draw water for Eliezer's camels, and there were ten of them. That initial action of hers, giving water to the camels, caught Eliezer's eye, and was an answer to his prayers. He had prayed that the woman who offered to give water to his camels would be the chosen of God.

Some of you may feel that you've been in what seems like a life-time of draining and devastating issues that have left you in a sort of permanent ten-day delay. Please remember: delay does not mean denial.

When Mary and Martha sent for Jesus to come to the bedside of their dying brother, Lazarus, Jesus said He would, and His disciples prepared to leave. But then, for some reason they could not understand, Jesus delayed His departure, and a few more days passed before His "yes" was manifested.

At times God waits until our situations become seemingly hopeless, and only then He manifests what He has already declared to be. When it seems that you'll never get the support you so desperately need from your loved one, know that your ten-day delay is nearly over. Now it's your time to be released to flow.

Some of you have fought discouraging circumstances for ten days, others for ten months, and still others for ten years. Whatever the case, now is your time to be released to flow.

Some of your loved ones may not want you to go after the plan of God for your life—even though they know and understand that you're anointed. They see your earrings and your bracelets. Even others standing by the well have come to the conclusion that the glow of the anointing is evident upon you, signifying to them that you've indeed been chosen by God. They all know that God is about to use you, and yet, as loving family members, they're afraid of where God might take you.

Finally, Rebekah's mother and her brother decided what the fair thing to do would be. "Let's ask Rebekah what *she* wants to do," they suggested.

In a very real sense, Rebekah was already connected with God. She had on His earrings to prove it. But even though she had already been chosen, her mighty anointing still could not take her anywhere. She first had to be released to flow by her precious family.

"Rebekah, do you want to go with this man?" they asked, hoping against hope that she would say no and wanting to give her an out. But she surprised them. "Yes," she replied. "I'll go."

Are You Ready?

Rebekah was ready to be released to flow into her destiny, which in this case was Isaac, the type of Jesus. He was her destiny.

The servant then essentially said to the family, "Did you hear what Rebekah said? She's ready to go." This was an important moment. It was not enough for Rebekah to be released by her family; she had to release herself. When she said, "I will go," she was essentially saying that she was giving up any other plans that she had made for herself in the past. She was ready to step out into the purpose set for her by God.

When you think about it, it's rather amazing that Rebekah answered as she did. After all, she had never laid eyes on Isaac. So she was saying "yes" to something totally unknown and unseen. But she was ready.

As you read this today, can you honestly say to God, "Yes, Lord, I want to be released to flow into my destiny," even though that destiny is still unknown and unseen? Can you say without any hesitation, "Yes, Lord, I'll go," even though you don't know for sure where He'll take you? Can you confidently tell Him, "Yes, Lord, I'll walk by faith, no matter where we end up"? Rebekah was ready:

And they called Rebekah, and said unto her, Wilt thou go with this man? And she said, I will go. And they sent away Rebekah their sister, and her nurse, and Abraham's servant, and his men.

Genesis 24:58-59

"Hanging" with those Who Are "Hooked"

After Rebekah declared that she was ready to be released to flow in her destiny, her family finally agreed and sent her on her way, even sending several handmaids and the family nurse to accompany her on the journey to her destiny. Can you grasp the significance of this entourage of hers?

Her anointing was tied to God, but her family now recognized it and released her to flow in her destiny by sending her away in the company of her nurse and her handmaidens. These left with Rebekah as she journeyed into her destiny.

Although Rebekah was the one who was chosen as the wife of destiny, the handmaidens had enough discernment to "hang" with the one who had been "hooked." And that's important. Learn to fellowship with people who have a special call on their lives. If you're expecting God to one day send for you with a call to destiny, in the meantime, maintain a relationship with those who have already answered His call.

"Hanging" with people who are always wandering here and there will only cause you to continue to wander, as well. "Hanging" with those who have been pulled from the dry desert of despair, defying the odds of failure, will cause a new level of faith to overtake you, as you anxiously await for your call to destiny.

Rebekah's obedience to the Lord and her willingness to exercise her faith released both her and her family to flow into the next dimension. And, in the process, others were released, and thus she did not journey off by herself into the sunset. She had people from home to go with her.

Daughter of God, He doesn't want you to be alone. That's why the Bible says that in the last days God will pour out His Spirit upon your sons and your daughters and even your handmaidens. He wants to anoint you, and

He also wants to bless your family, friends, and associates. He said:

And it shall come to pass afterward, that I will pour out my spirit upon all flesh; and your sons and your daughters shall prophesy, your old men shall dream dreams, your young men shall see visions.

Joel 2:28

The reason you need to pray for your sister and her release is that when she's released to flow, she'll need you to go with her. Rebekah was clearly not released to flow in her destiny alone. She went forth with company of others.

"The Mother of Thousands of Millions"

And they blessed Rebekah, and said unto her, Thou art our sister, be thou the mother of thousands of millions, and let thy seed possess the gate of those which hate them.

Genesis 24:60

Daughter of God, receive this revelation. Rebekah's entire family blessed her, prophetically declaring their blessing over her. Essentially, they said, "Rebekah, right now you're leaving as a sister, but we prophesy over your life that God will make you the mother to many."

Can we realize how huge this prophecy was? A thousand million is equivalent to one billion. So these family members were declaring that Rebekah would be the mother of more than a billion souls. This was all the more dramatic because it was uttered at a time when the concept of a billion people didn't yet exist in the earth.

There are many Rebekahs among us today, and it's very important for the Body of Christ to pray and intercede on behalf of those whom God has called to be used as vessels to birth others to their destiny. It is also important for us to be open to the prophetic word.

As you are released to flow into your destiny, be prepared to receive God's direction,

As you are released to flow into your destiny, be prepared to receive God's direction, His prophetic word, no matter how strange or impossible it may sound to you. There are people in place who will soon prophesy over you and declare, "You came as a sister, but you're leaving as a mother to millions." Never forget this story of Rebekah, and never forget the power of God to fulfill His fantastic promises.

When Rebekah's family members prophesied over her life, it wasn't just about their sister, her earrings, or the bracelets she now wore. Clearly, they now saw the hand of God in all of this. His great anointing was upon her life, and what they spoke was about all those whom she was called to bring to birth.

When you have completed this book and received the full revelation of it, people whom God has set in place will begin to prophesy mightily into your life, not because of what you have said, but because of what they will see in you. Heed those prophetic words, even if your mind cannot comprehend the vastness of God's plan for your life at the moment, as He lays it out through them.

Some of the most powerful words of prophecy that were spoken over my own life came at a time when I felt the furthest from God. Many words of prophecy came at a time when I was still struggling, trying to get free from bondages. Although I was not spiritually prepared to walk out the words at that particular time, I held onto each word of prophecy as a lifeline of hope that would somehow guide me through the times of darkness and confusion I was experiencing.

"Too Much" for Him?

There were several women at the well that day when Eliezer showed up, and of all of them, what was it about Rebekah that signaled to him that she was the chosen one? It was that the fact that she was busy. And in order to be noticed by the anointing, you must be willing to be found busy as well. God isn't calling any lazy people.

Rebekah was also willing to do something the other women wouldn't do. She went beyond what was required of her. This was exactly what Eliezer had prayed for. The woman God had chosen for Isaac's wife would go beyond what he required of her. He expressed it this way:

Behold, I stand by the well of water; and it shall come to pass, that when the virgin cometh forth to draw water, and I say to her, Give me, I pray thee, a little water of thy pitcher to drink; And she say to me, Both drink thou, and I will also draw for thy camels; let the same be the woman whom the Lord hath appointed out for my master's son.

Genesis 24:43-44

Can you imagine what must have been going through Eliezer's mind when we first saw Rebekah at the well *"with her pitcher on her shoulder"* (Genesis 24:45)? She was scooping water into that big, heavy clay pitcher. Then, when she saw Eliezer and he asked her for a drink, she provided him with water, not only for himself, but also for his multitude of camels. That was a lot of water.

In this way, Rebekah did much more than Eliezer had asked of her. He asked for a drink of water for Himself, but she could not help but supply water for the vehicles used to bring him to the well, the camels.

Rebekah probably made at least twenty trips to that well, going back and forth to water those camels. The other women who were standing around the well looked at her and probably laughed, saying, "Look at that dummy, Rebekah, watering those stupid camels for that stranger. We pretty girls don't do things like that."

But while they were laughing, they were totally unaware of the fact that Rebekah was literally fueling the very vehicle God would use to take her to her destiny. She would have the last laugh:

And Rebekah arose, and her damsels, and they rode upon the camels, and followed the man: and the servant took Rebekah, and went his way.

Genesis 24:61

Rebekah made a personal sacrifice to water the camels, and then she rode away on those very camels. That makes me want to shout!

Anytime you're doing something for the Lord in ministry, be it serving others, praying, giving, or whatever, don't let anyone tell you that you're doing far "too much."

Don't give in to the taunts of others. Your "too much" will be your transportation to your next divine step in God's plan.

Never feel that your labor is in vain. You're just putting gasoline in your vehicle. Some may laugh at you or your vehicle, but take heart. You're fueling the very thing that will carry you to your destiny.

A pastor once told me of a very beautiful story that illustrates this point. When he was still a young man in Bible college, he worked as a janitor around the college to help pay his school bills. One day, while cleaning the bathroom, he had a quick glimpse into the future, a sort of vision of his destiny. He suddenly thought, "This is a great school. I'm going to do the best job I can to keep it clean as long as I'm here. Who knows? Maybe some day God will give it to me." Little did he know that many years later he would purchase that very building and use it for his ministry. He was so glad then that he had taken good care of it when it was his responsibility to do so as a humble janitor.

My friends, never take the assignments that God allows you to walk in at certain times of your life as meaningless tasks or just a way to pass the time. Who knows? He may be allowing you to nurture the very thing that you will someday own or otherwise use.

The Scriptures teach:

For who hath despised the day of small things?

Zechariah 4:10

It's time for you to ride your camel. Ride whatever it takes for you to go beyond where you are today, as God begins to release you to flow into your destiny. Even if everybody is

114

laughing at you, refuse to give up. God will provide the vehicle to transport you to your place of destiny. Recognize today that He is releasing you to flow into it.

God sends your destiny your way in various forms. He then tests your reactions and your emotions toward your encounter with destiny. I remember being invited to preach at a very small ministry. On the day of the conference, a terrible storm arose. The weather was so bad that we couldn't see the road ahead of us. One of the young ladies with me suggested that maybe we should turn back. I replied, "For some reason, I feel that God wants us to continue." And we did.

We finally arrived at the church. I had known that it was a small ministry, but I hadn't known just how small. There were only five members, and three of them were on vacation at the time. Still, I knew there had to be a reason we had weathered the storm to be in that service.

Praise and worship came to an end, and nothing happened. I preached, and still nothing seemed to happen. I made an altar call, and someone from my own ministry came forward. I guess they didn't want me to think that my labor had been in vain.

As we were about to dismiss, a young couple came in the door of the church carrying a small child. When I looked at the child, I knew that something was about to happen. God had set us up for a miracle.

The Lord began to give me a word for that family. I was prompted to ask if the child might have been born with some disease. This seemed rather strange to me because the child seemed to be normal. But the mother began to cry and confirmed that it was true. "Something told us to come here," she said, "and that our child would be healed."

Immediately, I told them: "Your son will be able to hear, walk, and talk. He's totally healed."

That day, after I had prayed for the young family, I knew that God had allowed me to water my camel. At the time, that camel didn't look like much, but later, after that church had grown, it was transformed into an open door of divine destiny. Always remember in every situation to ask yourself a question, "Might this be a moment tied to a door in my destiny?"

Some of you who are reading this book will go far beyond where you believe God can take you. Start praising Him for that, and pray this simple declaration out loud:

Lord,

Thank You for releasing me to flow in my destiny. Thank You for drawing me in. Thank You for not letting me go.

I know that I'm chosen, and at this very moment I say 'yes' to You. No matter what vehicle You select for me, be it a camel or a car, a plane or a train, no matter who laughs at me or what they might say, I'm ready to be released to flow into my destiny.

Thank You, Lord, for loving me, and for transporting me to the next phase of my future.

Amen!

Essential Spiritual Ingredients
Power to perceive moments of opportunity

Chapter Eleven

The Sound of Approaching Destiny

CAPEHART'S CORNER: *Rejoice, for the sound of destiny is about to ring in the atmosphere with a seed of promise!*

As Rebekah was en route to Isaac, it's interesting to note what he was doing:

Isaac came from the way of the well Lahai-roi; for he dwelt in the south country.

Genesis 24:62

In essence, God was taking Rebekah from one well to another. In those dry lands, wells were the most important spots on the landscape. When you're thirsty and your body is dehydrated, when you're desperate, you need water, and you need it right away. Without water, one simply cannot survive.

In this passage, God symbolically brought Rebekah from one well (her source of physical water) to a new one (her source of spiritual water), and it was here that her new destiny would unfold in power. God will never draw you to your destiny without providing you with all that you need for your sustenance. In this case, Rebekah received "living water," and that living water would change her life forever.

A Godly Husband

As Rebekah neared the completion of her long journey, arriving at the Negev near Beerlahairoi, the Bible reports that Isaac was walking in the field, when suddenly he heard a sound on the night air. Your destiny is listening for the sound of your approach, so don't worry about the possibility of being overlooked.

And your destiny cannot make a mistake in this regard. It will come with a distinctive sound, one that will only connect with you like the final piece of a puzzle:

And Isaac went out to meditate in the field at the eventide: and he lifted up his eyes, and saw and, behold, the camels were coming.

Genesis 24:63

Isaac was a godly man. That's why he was in the field in the early evening. He was seeking God's direction for his life. Then, in the midst of his meditation, he heard a distant sound and looked up. He knew that sound, and he suddenly declared: "The camels are coming."

It's noteworthy that Isaac did not look up and say, "Here comes my future wife." His focus was the coming of the camels. He was Rebecca's destiny, but he didn't declare her arrival in his presence first. First, he heard the sound of what brought her to his presence.

Daughter of God, your destiny could be riding in on the very thing others have made fun of. It may be the area of ministry, or the skills and talents that you've refused to give up on. Others don't realize what you had "to water" to get to where you are today. You didn't realize that you were keeping it alive in order to keep yourself alive. Now, lift up your eyes toward heaven and behold. The camels are coming!

Of course, God appreciates your service and your worship. But to confound the wise, He will frequently release you to flow into your destiny on the very things others have laughed at. They thought them to be silly, stupid, or even hopeless. Only God knew their true worth.

Rebekah arrived at her destiny because she had faith enough in God to believe Him for a better place than the one she had been in before. Stop saying, "I've almost lost my mind," and trust God to take you to a better place, one where you can operate in a sound mind. Stop saying, "I almost killed myself," and trust God to provide you with "living water" at His spiritual well that never dries up. There, expect Him to provide you with constant hope in the midst of difficult circumstances. Stop saying, "I'm so discouraged about my ministry; nobody's standing with me," and start meditating on God, and listening for the sound of His camels that are even now approaching your life.

If you can trust God to carry you to a new place, you might quickly experience a divine turnaround in your ministry. You just may quickly find the perfect husband out praying in the field. It's your time.

Don't be afraid to take the risk, for you have nothing to lose. As long as you're tied to God, He'll never let you fail. You may temporarily fall, but He'll pick you up again. You're His chosen vessel, and there's an anointing upon your life. So, He wants you to ride your camel (your testimony or your struggle) to your divine destiny.

In the past, you may have been misunderstood because of your instinctive need to give camels a drink of water, your need to go beyond what was required of you in your walk with God. Rest assured that it's the sound of what you brought back to life in a desperate situation that will announce your arrival to others, a sound of joy that will ultimately catch the heart and attention of your connection in destiny.

Look Up and See God's Plan

When Rebekah looked up from her camel, she spotted Isaac approaching:

And Rebekah lifted up her eyes, and when she saw Isaac, she lighted off the camel.

Genesis 24:64

In that moment, Rebekah was seeing for the first time the man destined to be her husband. He was waiting for her, and she was so excited that she *"lighted off the camel."* That action was symbolic of the fact that she had finally reached the next step in God's divine plan, as she was drawn to her new destiny. She got off the camel and embraced destiny.

In time, you'll have to get off the camel and embrace destiny too. What brought you to your place of destiny will be kindly remembered, but it won't be needed to keep you there.

In effect, Rebekah was drawn, or carried, to her destiny through the vessel of a big, ugly animal. (I apologize to camel lovers everywhere, but I wouldn't want to kiss one of them. And have you ever smelled their breath? It's absolutely atrocious!).

The Immediate Rewards

Now, let's look at the immediate rewards for Rebekah's faith and willingness to obey God:

And Isaac brought her into his mother Sarah's tent, and took Rebekah, and she became his wife; and he loved her: and Isaac was comforted after his mother's death.

Genesis 24:67

Do you see what's happening here? Once Rebekah took her step of faith and climbed onto that camel to journey to Isaac's land, God blessed her, and she became the wife of a godly man, one who prayed, sought God, and *"loved her"* dearly.

And Rebekah did her part. God used her presence to comfort Isaac, her husband. He was still experiencing sorrow for having lost his mother three years earlier.

Barren and Birthing

Clearly, God's hand was upon Rebekah's life, but that didn't exempt her from future challenges and disappointments. While she received some immediate rewards when she arrived in Isaac's camp, there were still some very significant struggles to come.

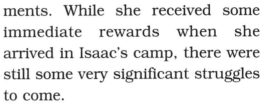

Walking in your destiny doesn't mean that your entire purpose will be manifested immediately.

Imagine her joy at being led by God to the new land to join forces with her new husband! Imagine her joy when she recounted to others what God had done in her life! And, imagine her extreme disappointment when, for the next nineteen years, she proved to be barren, unable to start the family that Isaac had so long hoped and prayed for.

Walking in your destiny doesn't mean that your entire purpose will be manifested immediately. Many become discouraged when they arrive at their destiny, only to experience a period of barrenness and a time of unfruitful production.

Don't leave your destined place broken because you're faced with a moment of barrenness. Prepare yourself to continue to wait. Look at it this way: You waited for years before you were placed in a position to produce. Certainly, you can now wait until your position starts producing.

Rebekah may have been barren for the moment, but she had a word of prophecy that had been spoken over her life by her family, and it said that she would indeed produce. I feel your heart gasping now, as you're saying, "What do you do when you've been given a word that God would make you the mother of billions, and you can't even be the mother of one?"

The lesson is clear here. You can be squarely in God's will, doing precisely what He wants you to do, going precisely where He wants you to go, and still experience long periods of barrenness and fruitlessness.

During the years that Rebekah was barren, Isaac persistently appealed to God in prayer for a son. Finally, God heard his cry. Rebekah became pregnant and bore Isaac twins. They called them Esau and Jacob.

No matter how barren your current circumstances might seem, no matter how many are laughing at you, if you're seeking God and know that you're in His will, then trust Him that, in due time, you'll birth precisely the plan God has for your life. In Rebekah's case, she birthed not just one son; God gave her two sons. He would use those two children to make Rebekah the mother of two great nations.

Think about this. Nineteen years before Rebekah gave birth to Esau and Jacob, she received the prophecy from her family which essentially said, "You'll be the mother of more than a billion souls." One can only wonder if during those nineteen years of being barren, she didn't occasionally say to herself, "Yeah, right! I can't even produce one kid, let alone mother a heritage of thousands of millions." But God is always faithful to His Word.

"Rebekahs, look up. The camels are coming. Yes, others are laughing at you now, but you'll be the mother of thousands of millions. So don't fret. Trust and rest in My Word."

125

The Seed of Promise

God assured Rebekah that she would become the mother of two great nations, and that *"the elder [would] serve the younger"* (Genesis 25:23). The apostle Paul later wrote that Rebekah's struggle was used by God to demonstrate that the choice of *"the children of promise"* depends entirely on God, not on our own will:

> *Not as though the word of God hath taken none effect. For they are not all Israel, which are of Israel: Neither, because they are the seed of Abraham, are they all children: but In Isaac shall they seed be called. That is, They which are the children of the flesh, these are not the children of God: but the children of the promise are counted for the seed. For this is the word of promise, At this time will I come, and Sara shall have a son.*

> *And not only this; but when Rebecca also had conceived by one, even by our father Isaac; (For the children being not yet born, neither having done any good or evil, that the purpose of God according to election might stand, not of works, but of him that calleth;) It was said unto her, The elder shall serve the younger.*

> *Romans 9:6-12*

Daughter of God, as you encounter the current situations in your life, remember that the Word of God will always prevail. Never think that *"the word of God hath taken none effect,"* because *"the children of promise are counted for the seed."*

126

God's Word will always come to pass, even if nineteen years have gone by in the interim. So, fear not, and faint not. The camels are coming!

Essential Spiritual Ingredients
The strength to savor the sudden sounds of destiny

Chapter Twelve

The Footprints of Faith

CAPEHART'S CORNER: *The enemy may not be able to find a gravestone with your name on it, marking your past defeat, but he can find tracks where you walked out your past!*

"There Are No Graves"

*A*ccepting the fact that God has a plan of destiny for your life is easy, and believing that you can reach that destiny is even easier. But getting up by faith and taking the steps to get there can seem difficult, sometimes even impossible. Usually, the first thing that will come to your mind is, "What if I don't make it? What if I fail in this? What if the enemy completely destroys me while I'm in the midst of this faith walk?" And he will surely try.

After the children of Israel had left Egypt, they suddenly found themselves in a situation that appeared to make them a bull's-eye for enemy target practice (see Exodus 13 and 14). God had allowed them to be released from the bondage of Pharaoh and had sent them on a journey to destiny by way of the wilderness. But it didn't take the children of Israel long to begin to complain about their uncertain walk to destiny, and they longed for the familiar tastes of bondage. Then they wanted to know why God had led them by way of the wilderness.

God's answer was that He had not sent them through the wilderness to harm them, but to help them (see Exodus 13:17). If they were confronted with war, they might change their minds about how wonderful freedom was and actually return to Egypt. Today, you must understand that God will always send you down a path of escape designed in such a way that even if you became afraid and wanted to turn around, you would not be able to find your way back. God's plan is to get you to a point of no return. He wants you to always go forward, never backward.

You must get to the place in God that you declare, "I don't know what lies ahead, but I know that I can no longer go back."

And when Pharaoh drew nigh, the children of Israel lifted up their eyes, and, behold, the Egyptians marched after them; and they were sore afraid: and the children of Israel cried out unto the Lord. And they said unto Moses, Because there were no graves in Egypt, hast thou taken us away to die in the wilderness? wherefore hast thou dealt thus with us, to carry us forth out of Egypt?

Exodus 14:10-11

When the children of Israel made the statement *"because there were no graves in Egypt,"* they were being sarcastic. It seemed to them, at the time, that they were surely about to die. But I find something very powerful in their words, something very true. In a sense what they said was even prophetic. Perhaps there were graves in Egypt, but not *their* graves. The enemy had failed in his desire to destroy them in captivity. They had survived it.

And if the enemy had not been able to destroy them when they were under his authority, what did they now have to fear when they were under the shadow of the Almighty? In the same way, if the enemy was not able to destroy your reputation, your health, your family, your finances, or your mind when you were making all the wrong decisions for your life (without benefit of the guidance of the Lord), what makes you think that he can ruin you now that God is in control of everything that you do? He cannot.

The Walk Out

There was not much left in Egypt as a reminder that the children of Israel had once been there, and that was good. Of course, God wants you to be able to remember that you have a past, but He also wants you to understand that you've survived your past, and you're surviving the present struggles in the wilderness.

If there was no grave to mark your place in bondage, then what does God leave as a sign that you have made it through? I'm convinced that all the enemy can find are the tracks where you walked out your past. And if there was no grave for you in the bondage, then there are no grave clothes to be found and no stink of death.

131

In Daniel's day, the three Hebrew boys where thrown into the fiery furnace (see Daniel 3). When they were released from the fiery furnace, after being expected to die there, something was immediately noticeable about them. Their clothes bore no smell of the fire; there was no stench on them.

The burning fire of the Babylonian furnaces had no power over these men. They came out of them with a testimony of life: They had left no grave in the furnace, just footprints. This meant that they had been there, but they hadn't stayed there.

As God begins to draw you closer to your destiny, people will often remind you of where you came from. The enemy will also attempt to keep your mind reminiscing over the failures of the past. But the New Testament declares:

If any man be in Christ, he is a new creature: old things are passed away; behold, all things are become new.

2 Corinthians 5:17

Let this mind be in you, which was also in Christ Jesus.

Philippians 2:5

You're a new person, so use your new mind of Christ to meditate daily on the plan that God has for your life. Even when you do look back and wonder how you made it through, simply look down, and you'll see a set of footprints that you've left.

If you look long enough, you'll discover that the footprints may have started out being a set of one, yours alone, only to turn into a set of two, when Jesus began to walk with you.

"But I have noticed that even the set of two footprints disappeared," someone might say. That was the day the Lord picked you up and carried you out of bondage. You could not make it on your own.

Never worry about the things you may have to encounter in your walk to destiny by way of the wilderness. You will not come out smelling like what you went through.

The Stairs of Strength

A few years ago I had an awesome prophetic experience that changed my life and increased my faith to walk out my destiny in God's timing. It happened in the following way.

You will not come out smelling like what you went through.

I was invited to attend a prayer presbytery, where prophets gather to speak into the lives of those willing to listen to words of direction given specifically for them. At the time, I was not at all familiar with this approach to the prophetic, although God was using me in the prophetic realm. After careful consideration, I chose not to participate in the presbytery.

Just before the prophets were about to end their session, someone came to me and said, "Please, I really believe you should go in." I walked to the back of the church and entered a small room filled with prophets and prophetesses basking in the presence of the Lord. There was a gleam of God's glory on their faces. I wondered if they could all tell that I was not at all comfortable with the idea.

Within moments, a young man, who identified himself as a prophet from Atlanta, Georgia, began to tell me that the Lord had sent me there to receive a word from Him. As he began to speak, I immediately felt the presence of the Lord overtake me.

He said, "Daughter think it not strange that I allowed you to see an open door and experience the joy of the view and not allow you to walk through it. You see, what you think is a door slammed shut by the enemy is really a door opened by destiny."

He went on to confirm a very serious situation I had just faced in my ministry. God had allowed me to experience something that I fully expected to be an overnight success, but it had turned into an instant fizzle, and it had been done publicly. God let me know through that young man that He knew all about it.

The next words that the young prophet spoke truly changed my life. He stated that it was not the will of God for me to become an overnight success in ministry, but it was His will that I maintain a lifetime of mounting success. He explained it like this, "God has decided for you not to take the elevator ride to the high places in Him. Instead, He has placed you on the stairs. By taking the stairs, it will take you much longer to reach your destination, but you'll learn so much more about God in your walk up that others seem to never learn on the quick elevator ride. Although the elevator ride would cause you to get to your destination at a much faster pace, once you arrived, you would quickly discover that you were not prepared to stay in the race. Your walk on the stairs will cause you to become very tired and weary at times, but it is in these times that you will learn to rest and trust in the strength of God." The more the man spoke, the greater the presence of the Lord became, and I soon found myself on the floor weeping in God's presence.

The prophet finally concluded: "God will allow you to have a powerful experience on the stairs. Each step will teach you a great principle that will become an important foundation for the future, the time when you finally stand in your destiny. When he had finished, someone handed me an audio recording of the entire powerful prophetic word, and I was able to review it periodically and learn more.

At pivotal points in my life, I began to take steps toward my God-ordained destiny, and I realized that the prophecy was true. The steps are not always easy, but the lessons of life presented on the stairs can bring an awesome assurance of the anointing that awaits us in our future.

Recently, I left my room in a hotel and was on my way down to the lobby. Of course, I took the elevator. Although this word of prophecy had been given to me a few years ago, it was only at that moment that the words about the stairs became clear to me.

As I approached the elevator that day, my eyes locked onto a sign posted alongside it. It read, "In case of a fire, take the stairs." Tears begin to stream down my face as I heard the voice of the Lord speaking to me. He said, "You see, when there's a fire, you can get stuck on the elevator and lose your life, but if you're caught in a fire on the stairs, you can simply keep on running." What a powerful word that was from the Lord! If you find yourself with a decision to make about how fast you want to arrive at your destiny, you may want to consider the stairs. It may take you longer, but in case of a fiery trial, you can simply keep on running.

The Guiding Light

God gave the Israelites a light to guide them, and a guiding light will always be present to lead you to your path of purpose:

And the Lord went before them [the children of Israel] by day in a pillar of a cloud, to lead them the way; and by night in a pillar of fire, to give them light; to go by day and night.

Exodus 13:21

You're not expected to know the way. You're only expected to follow the path through the way that has already been made for you. David exulted:

Thy word is a lamp unto my feet, and a light unto my path.

Psalm 119:105

God instructed Moses to tell the children of Israel:

Stand still, and see the salvation of the Lord, which he will shew to you to day: for the Egyptians whom ye have seen to day, ye shall see them again no more for ever.

Exodus 14:13

In the midst of God bringing you out, He's not expecting you to fight. He wants you to simply stand still and watch Him move on your behalf. He'll lead you out by guiding your every step.

Many fall because they have sought instruction and guidance from those who don't have the roadmap for their particular life or the blueprint for their particular design. Be extremely careful when you're in need of divine direction.

Lead by Example

Make sure that the person speaking into your life concerning the next move is someone whom God has placed in your life as a guiding light. It's always a good idea to have someone to look up to, someone to mentor you in the Body of Christ. Just make sure that you're looking up to the right person.

The person who should be a mentor to your life should be a leader by example. They should not only be able to tell you how to get to your destiny; they should also be able to show you.

Be very prayerful about spiritual mentors. Your spiritual mentor should be someone who possesses the same type of anointing that rests upon your own life. A mentor is not someone you mimic, but someone who gives you the guidance, counsel, and leadership needed to get you to your destiny.

Not Without a Fight

The word of the Lord to the children of Israel was that the Egyptians they were seeing that day would not be seen by them again. Once God starts fighting on your behalf, the stronghold of the enemy will suddenly fall. Make sure that you're ready to release every stronghold when God starts fighting your battle. He plays for keeps, and He goes for the kill.

As Pharaoh's army drew closer to the children of Israel, something wonderful happened:

The angel of God, which went before the camp of Israel, removed and went behind them; and the pillar of the cloud went from before their face, and stood behind them: And it came between the camp of the Egyptians and the camp of Israel; and it was a cloud and darkness to them, but it gave light by night to these: so that the one came not near the other all night.

Exodus 14:19-20

When God is leading you out, He goes in front of you, but when He's destroying the enemy, He goes behind you. What the enemy sees as darkness in your life is God's illuminating glory shielding you. The power of His light is for your guidance through the wilderness.

The Lord instructed Moses to tell the Israelites to turn back and encamp near a place called Pihahiroth, between Migdol and the sea, directly opposite Baalzephon. Pharaoh would think that they were simply wandering around the land in confusion, being hemmed in by the desert (see Exodus 14:1-3). Often God does the very same thing in our lives. He makes it appear to the enemy that you're totally lost, that your situation has shut you in and caused you to experience a state of confusion. And it works.

But you're not lost, you're not confused, you're not crazy, you haven't lost control, you're not unstable, and you're not sinking. It's all a setup to fool the enemy. God is working on your behalf to show the enemy that he's decided to attack the wrong person. You will come out of this experience with a testimony that says, "Although you've seen me encounter many adversities, you've never seen one of them overtake me." Learn to trust God, no matter what. Then, step back, and let Him do the work for you.

The Road to Success

I was recently visiting my hometown, Graceville, Florida, a very small town, when I noticed a sign that read, "The road to success is always under construction." What a true statement that is. Although you may be on the road to success, you'll always be under construction. God's always preparing you daily to handle the pressure, the problem, the pain, and the power that comes with His anointing upon your life. Be prepared to live a lifestyle that bears for life a sign which reads "Under Construction."

Essential Spiritual Ingredients
Steps of strength toward a strong stand

Chapter Thirteen

The Wait is Finally Over

CAPEHART'S CORNER: *When you begin to soar in the high places of God, you will begin to experience visions and dreams like never before!*

But they that wait upon the Lord shall renew their strength; they shall mount up with wings as eagles; they shall run, and not be weary; and they shall walk, and not faint.

Isaiah 40:31

In my early adult walk, I was probably one of the most impatient people you could ever meet. I wanted everything to happen now. When my husband and I decided to have a home built, I expected it to be completed in a month

141

or less. I would say, "What do you mean they're not finished yet? What do you mean they have to wait until this dries or that settles?" My lack of patience was also exhibited in my reaction to office workers, store clerks, and anyone whom I felt lacked the proper speed. My favorite reaction, when things were not moving as fast as I thought they should, was to lash out with the words, "Never mind! I'll do it myself!"

Of course, I never wanted to admit that each time I chose speed over quality, I made an absolute mess of things. Although there are many skills that I've been blessed with, there are many more that I lack. There are so many things I have no clue about finishing, let alone starting. But I couldn't stand to wait on anyone or anything.

When I would hear the words, "It will happen; just wait," it seemed to send my nerves into a tightened fit." But through years of refusing to wait and then having to suffer the consequences of my quick reactions, I finally learned to wait on God's timing for my life.

Expect to Wait

My Soul, wait thou only upon God; for my expectation is from him.

Psalm 62:5

Reaching your predestined goals in God will not happen overnight. In fact, I've come to the conclusion that the saying "good things happen for those who wait" is really true.

What does it mean to wait on God? The Bible dictionary's definition of the word *wait* is "to set oneself to expect

142

God to move." Another definition is "to remain in readiness for some action." Each day, you should be prepared with expectation for God to move on your behalf.

Waiting can be a long, lonely path. It can be a time when the world seems to have stopped turning. It can appear to be a dark, dreary bottomless pit. But be assured waiting builds your level of trust in God.

Don't allow bad situations to change your attitude of expectation.

Don't allow bad situations to change your attitude of expectation. Never allow yourself to complain or make foolish decisions in an attempt to make things happen sooner. Complaining and trust can never rest in the same heart.

No matter what it looks like, stand on the promise of God. Even if you have to stand on His promise in the midst of an ocean surrounded by sharks, just waiting on your faith to fail, hold on to the expectation of knowing that God will answer you.

Abraham's wait for his promise is a great example to us, as believers, of the power of waiting. Although God had given him a promise of an heir, it was twenty-five years later before that promise came to pass. Are you willing to wait on God by expecting Him to answer, even if it takes twenty-five years?

As you wait, there will be days when you'll feel that God has forgotten that you're still waiting. You may also feel that you've waited for so long that you yourself have forgotten what you were waiting on. Keep waiting. God is faithful.

Wait on the Lord: be of good courage, and he shall strengthen thine heart: wait, I say, on the Lord.

Psalm 27:14

Mount Up with Wings as Eagles

But those who wait on the Lord shall renew their strength; they shall mount up with wings like eagles, they shall run and not be weary, they shall walk and not faint.

Isaiah 40:31, NKJ

I've read Isaiah 40:31 time and time again throughout my Christian walk, and I've also found myself quoting it during times when it felt like I didn't have the strength to go on. But I can never forget the day the Lord instructed me to read this scripture and then asked me what it meant to my life. I found that I had no real understanding of the depth of meaning in this scripture, and then God set me on a search to learn why He had compared a Christian's personality and strength to that of eagles throughout the Scriptures.

My journey of understanding would take me through mountains of research and countless hours of reading on the habits of eagles, and I was overwhelmed as I reflected on the many situations in my life that related to their lifestyle. One process in particular caught my attention early in my research, the process of young eagles preparing to fly. This process is known as fledging.

When an eagle is fledging, he has developed the necessary feathers to fly, but still he must be prepared to fly, and he must be taught to fly. Eagles are born to fly, but unless they're properly prepared for it and actually taught to do it, they'll never be able to reach their potential to soar above the clouds.

It's the same in your walk to destiny. You were born and created to soar in the high places of God, but you must first be prepared and taught. And that's truly not an overnight process; it requires a discipline for learning.

When the fledging process begins, the baby eagle is too fat to fly and must first eliminate the excess weight before it will be able to take to the air. The mother and father eagle are not nearly as impressed with the beautiful feathers their son has sprouted as he is. They know that he can fly, and they hope that he will fly, but it's not a foregone conclusion. They set about to implement the arduous task of preparing their baby to do what he was created to do.

Before the birth of the baby eaglet, the nest was prepared with a nice comfortable cushion made from the mother's soft feathers. Then, once he was born, each day he was supplied with sufficient food in the comfort of that nice environment. But when the fledging process begins, the warm and comfortable cushion is suddenly removed, and the food stops coming.

Now, the once comfortable home of the baby eagle has suddenly become a place of confusion and despair. Something that he has come to count on day after day is suddenly gone. His comfort is no more, and the pleasure of his mother and father running to answer his every beck and call is frustrated. He suddenly finds himself abandoned, alone, and in a very uncomfortable place.

To the eaglet, it must appear that his parents have deserted him, but that's not the case. They understand the process. If they don't remove the comfort of his resting place and force him to become very hungry for what he needs, he will never lose the excess fat and gather the strength and determination to get up and go after the reason he was created.

An eaglet was not created to sit in a comfortable nest all day long, being supplied by the daily catches of food brought to him by his parents. He was created to soar with the wind, and to hunt for himself.

After denying her little one food for a long period of time, allowing some of his excess fat to be eliminated and making him very hungry, the mother eagle will fly over the nest with just what he longs for, a nice fat worm. She flies close enough to the nest for him to see it and yet far enough away so that he cannot reach it. This causes him to get up and jump, to try to get to his food. This jumping is part of the process, as it causes him to loose more of the excess fat, and it also strengthens him.

Have you noticed some things in your life that seemed to hinder you from obtaining the plan of God? Has there been a time when you could actually see your destiny, but were frustrated because you couldn't quite reach it? Did it cause you to get up and begin to jump in your spirit for a breakthrough? This was the time that God was causing your spirit to be enlarged. He was stretching your faith, increasing your passion, and giving you a hunger to go after His plan for your life.

When God removes your comfort, it may appear that He's punishing you or that He's forgotten you. But no, He's simply preparing you to finally do what you've been created to do. Like the eagle, you were created to soar.

He Won't Let You Fall

In the final stage of the fledging process, the mother eagle actually pushes the baby eaglet out of the nest. This sends the small one into a spiraling downward fall and must be a terrifying experience. In the meantime, the father eagle is flying overhead, maintaining a constant view of the baby's progress.

He found him in a desert land, and in the waste howling wilderness; he led him about, he instructed him, he kept him as the apple of his eye. As an eagle stirreth up her nest, fluttereth over her young, spreadeth abroad her wings, taketh them, beareth them on her wings: So the Lord alone did lead him, and there was no strange god with him. He made him ride on the high places of the earth, that he might eat the increase of the fields.

Deuteronomy 32:10-13

As the baby eagle spirals helplessly toward death, can you imagine the anguish and disappointment? He struggles, trying to understand why this is happening to him. When he cries out for help, he seems to be totally ignored and continues to fall. But we have the promise:

Now unto him that is able to keep you from falling, and to present you faultless before the presence of his glory with exceeding joy ...

Jude 24

Suddenly, just before the baby eagle hits the rocky bottom, his father swoops down, takes him up on his wings, and returns him back to the nest. Mary Whelchel wrote: "An eaglet cannot fall faster than his father can fly."[1] That's a comforting thought.

Alas, when the father eagle returns his little one back to the nest, it is not to find comfort and to eat at last, but to allow the mother eagle to throw him out again. This process continues until the baby eagle has what I call a defining moment, a moment of understanding what it is that his parents are trying to get him to do. Many times, when God is trying to get you to go to the next step in your destiny, He'll allow you to go through certain situations that will teach you vital lessons for the flight to your future. It is a trying moment, but it can become a defining moment.

Sooner or later, after several times of being pushed from the nest, then rescued and returned to the nest, the baby eagle finally realizes that it's not the art of falling his parents are trying to teach him; it's the ability to reach inside himself and use his predetermined gifts of soaring to succeed. At some point, the baby eagle discovers his wings and begins to flap them, gaining strength and ability in the process. Before long, he is flying, and soon it will seem as if he has done it all of his life.

When the little one has finally begun to fly, the mother and father eagle are overcome with excitement, not because they feel that they've taught the baby well, but, more so, because he's excelling in what he's been taught. During this

1. Mary Whelchel, Soaring on High, Spiritual Insights From the Life of an Eagle (Chicago, Illinois: Moody Press, 2001),pg 45

rejoicing, they soar through the sky, their wings touching each other. This is their time of celebration and it notifies all other eagles: "Our baby has learned to soar."

Once you begin to soar in the high places of God, you'll begin to experience visions and dreams like never before.

It's Time to Soar

To *soar* means "to glide high in the sky." It also means "to rise in thought and imagination, to rise in spirit far above the common and usual level." Can you imagine how God the Father and our Lord Jesus Christ feel when we begin to soar? I'm convinced that a celebration takes place in the heavenlies, as our Father and Jesus declare to others that we've not fallen as we thought we would. We did not die, although we thought we were on our way down. All of heaven rejoices when you soar!

Once you begin to soar in the high places of God, you'll begin to experience visions and dreams like never before. During this time, it's a good idea to keep a journal. As the dreams and visions began to flood your spirit, you can make notes to yourself about them. I also recommend to everyone that they keep a small tape (or digital) recorder handy. I've found that when your spirit begins to soar, revelations will come to you so rapidly that even knowing shorthand will not equip you to capture it all on paper.

Life Without the Wind

Why are we not soaring in the level God has created us for? The Lord showed me something concerning the eagle that literally made me shout, weep, and travail for the Body of Christ. About midway through an eagle's life, it can experience a chemical imbalance and go through something called the molting process. It is a very unusual occurrence that can teach us a lot about ourselves.

The molting process seems to hit the eagle from out of nowhere, and during this process an eagle, which is accustomed to soaring, will suddenly find itself feeling helpless, no longer possessing the strength to soar. A molting eagle will go from soaring above the clouds to hiding in a secluded area behind the rocks. It will go from lifting its head up high to sitting with its head in a downward position.

When this happens, the eagle must be wondering, "Why am I here? I'm an eagle, and so I'm supposed to be soaring. I'm not supposed to be in the valley. I was created to soar over the mountaintops."

During molting, an eagle's tear ducts dry up. Does this sound familiar to anyone? When you've cried all you can cry, and now you don't have any more tears to cry, you can understand the eagle.

The eagle begins to lose weight as his strength diminishes, and his beak and talons become useless for hunting and tearing the flesh of any prey. The chemical imbalance he has suffered causes calcium to build up on his talons and beak. He beats them against the rocks until they actually fall off. Unless they can be restored, he can never hunt again.

His vision also weakens, and, for some odd reason, he begins to pull out his own feathers. Not only does he no longer have a desire to fly; he is quickly losing the ability to fly.

Understandably, many eagles don't survive this process, and the more I study this awesome process, the more compassion I feel for many in the Body of Christ who are weakened, sidelined, and in danger of extinction.

Birds of a Feather

As an eagle is going through this molting process, it sits in the valley, not flying, and therefore, not eating. Other eagles, going through the same process, gather around them. Together, they sit in the warmth of the sun, trying to conserve their strength.

We're a lot like that. Misery loves company, and those of us who are going through similar trials are often drawn to each other. But that's dangerous. How can you come out of a state of discouragement if you only have fellowship with people who are discouraged themselves?

Thank God for intercessors who refuse to allow us to die! In time, older eagles will gather around those that are molting and will support them. They seem to understand what the molting eagles are going through, perhaps because they've been through it themselves. In Christian terms, they've not come to criticize or complain, but to speak life and to succor the weaker ones among them.

This is not immediately apparent to the suffering eagles. Because the older eagles gather in the air above them, flying back and forth, screaming as they go, this must seem to the molting eagles as if the others have come to mock them in their misery and depression. To their surprise and delight, they find that the older eagles are dropping food down to them. What a joy it must be to the molting eagles to know that the others have not come to mock them, but to help them! They have been missed, and the other eagles have gotten together to search for them.

How many of us in the Body of Christ have noticed that someone is missing and not soaring with us as usual, and yet we fail to go looking for them? We know that we've not seen Sister What's-Her-Name at Bible study, Sunday school, or church. Maybe we've noticed that they're not soaring in the Spirit the way they used to. They're not as excited about worship as they once were. How many times have we gotten together to go look for some molting saint?

Eagles are generally loners, but amazingly, at this time, they come together for the purpose of restoring the molting ones back to the fold. What a wonderful example for all of us!

As the older eagles continue to drop food, the molting eagles slowly begin to eat again and to gain weight. If they can have enough time in the sun, if they can simply wait long enough in the presence of the sunlight (or Son-light, in our case) without giving up, they'll eventually begin to be renewed. Their feathers, beak, and talons will all grow back, and the eagle will be able to soar again, now with even greater strength.

This whole process takes about forty days, and during that time, molting eagles stay hidden in the rocks until their strength has been renewed, and until their pain is gone. In Christian terms, they stay there until they can stop worrying about who's talking about them and who doesn't like them. They must refuse to let a forty-day trial cause them to die. They must refuse to let any test keep them from ever soaring again.

The older eagles are faithful to stay around until they see the molting eagles come from behind the rocks. They will continue to intercede and do their part right up to the moment they see the molting eagle mount up with wings, as if to say, "I know you thought I was dead, but I'm back! I know you thought I would give up, but I'm still in the race! You thought I would lose my mind, but I came back to let you know something. Not only have I not lost my own mind; but in the process, I've gained the mind of Christ!"

The prophet Micah declared:

Rejoice not against me, O mine enemy: when I fall I shall arise; when I sit in darkness, the Lord shall be a light unto me.

Micah 7:8

Once the renewed eagle mounts up, the other eagles leave, knowing that the weakened one has been restored back to its rightful place. No matter how bad you were hurt, keep eating the morsels supplied to you. If your husband left you, keep eating the morsels (representing healing and renewal) that those who have been where you are now and have survived it are dropping into your spirit. Keep eating until your strength has returned.

The Church as a whole is hurting in this area. We don't have nearly enough people soaring above us when something hinders us. When was the last time you know of some eagles who got together to tell the devil, "You will not have our sister (or brother); we will wait in the wind until they come back to us"?

"Prophesy to the Wind"

When God spoke this to me, I got up, because I wanted to hear more. "The wind" ... what was God talking about?

I saw in the book of Ezekiel (37:9) that the Lord had told the prophet to *"prophesy to the wind."* He said to me now,

"Prophesy to the wind that it may bring life back to every eagle that has found itself in this condition."

I felt a great urgency in my spirit to get an understanding of what God was saying. So I continued to read:

As an eagle stirreth up her nest, fluttereth over her young, spreadeth abroad her wings, taketh them, beareth them on her wings …

Deuteronomy 32:11

This word *fluttereth* means "to move over." God fluttered, or *"moved upon the face of the waters"* (Genesis 1:2). In Hebrew, the word *fluttereth*, or moves, is *ruach*, and there is much debate over whether this word *ruach* means "spirit" or "wind." For our purposes, we will use both of them. Our Ruach is both wind and Spirit.

The Amazing Names

While reading about the life of eagles I discovered that the U.S. National Eagle Repository is located in Denver, Colorado, which is where all dead and wounded eagles are sent from around the country. This repository is protected by the federal government. I began to feel that the Lord had set me up for something wonderful, and it happened.

While I was studying for this word, the Lord made it possible for me to receive an invitation to preach at Bishop Dennis Leonard's church. The week before I was to go to the church, I received a phone call from Bishop John Francis in London, England. Bishop Francis said the Lord had told him that I was to minister in his church the following Sunday. I was free, so I agreed to go.

I was quickly reminded of a word the Lord had spoken to me earlier: "I will show you in the natural what I'm about to do in the Spirit." I later learned that the name of Bishop Francis' church in London was Ruach Ministries. Not only that, Bishop Leonard's church is located in Denver, Colorado. I knew then that God had sent me this word on the eagles in season, so that I could tell all dead and wounded eagles about the hope to be renewed and again soar.

The Lord sent me to Ruach Ministries in London, to be in the presence of the wind, so that I would be able to carry it with me to Denver, the location for all dead and wounded eagles. There, I preached a message entitled "It's Time to Soar Again," and it seemed to all come together.

As I completed my study on the eagles, the Lord spoke to me and said, "This revelation will change you forever. When it's all said and done, no matter what the eagles have gone through, no matter what sent them to the burial field or the wounded valley, in the end, they will be standing where their heritage is.

If nothing else has gotten your spirit turning, this, I'm confident will. The name of Bishop Leonard's church is Heritage Christian Center. It took everything in me to stand upright and be able to minister this word to his congregation. How great is our God!

Safety Under His Wings

Eagles are sent to the repository at Denver for various reasons, and there they are kept under lock and key. Some are sent because they've come in contact with high tension electric lines and have been shocked so badly that they don't survive or barely survive. Some are sent because they collide with something bigger than themselves, something so big, and yet they didn't see it coming. It just seemed to come out of nowhere. Either they don't survive it, or they're left severely wounded.

Then there are those who've been poisoned. They ate something contaminated, and the poison began to destroy every cell in their bodies. Some survive and are sent for recovery, and others don't survive it at all.

And finally, there are those that have been shot by hunters. They go from soaring in the sky one minute to lying prostrate on the ground without the strength or the will to get up the next. Some survive, and many do not.

As I was learning all of this, questions flooded my mind. Why would eagles be kept under lock and key—even after they're dead? Why would anyone hunt and kill an eagle? And, again, why has God compared Christians to eagles? Slowly, the answers began to come.

Eagles are kept under lock and key even after they're dead because, even then, they're still valuable. God wants you to know that you may have experienced some things that have knocked the breath out of you and taken the wind out of your spirit. This may have caused you to die prematurely, but you're still valuable to God. He will set you in a place of safekeeping:

Be merciful unto me, O God, be merciful unto me: for my soul trusteth in thee: yea, in the shadow of thy wings will I make my refuge, until these calamities be overpast.

Psalm 57:1

Eagles are hunted because they're valuable, and the enemy will try to shoot you out of the sky because of the anointing on your life. He won't just sit back and watch you soar to the place where God has created you to be. He'll try any-thing to stop you any way he can. When you become victorious in your obedience to God, you become a threat to him and his kingdom. *"Endure unto the end"*:

Christians are compared to eagles because of the awesome lessons of strength and courage that can be gained by observing the life of eagles.

ᗯ ᗯ

But he that shall endure unto the end, the same shall be saved.

Matthew 24:13

Christians are compared to eagles because of the awesome lessons of strength and courage that can be gained by observing the life of eagles. The Lord showed me, for example, that an eagle does not require a jumpstart or a runway. All he has to do is spread his wings and let the wind take him up.

He made him ride on the high places of the earth.

Deuteronomy 32:13

If God has made you *"ride,"* you must keep in mind that if you're riding, then you're not driving. God's driving, and therefore He knows the directions. Sit back and enjoy the ride to your high places.

Your high place is your place of purpose. As you begin to fulfill the assignment of God on your life, it will cause

157

you to begin to eat out of the increase of your fields. As you obey the plan of God for your life, you'll begin to experience a level of growth and prosperity in every area. Enjoy the ride, as God takes you to your high places in Him.

I've learned a very valuable lesson through all of this. No matter how tough a trial may be or how long you have to go through something, just hang on. Help is on the way.

Eagles, I now prophesy to you that it's time to soar again. As you begin to feel the wind of God beneath your wings, remember that you don't need a runway. The moment you feel the wind, you're ready to soar.

As you embrace your final pull to destiny, know that your search is over. Your molting process is also over. God has prepared a wonderful plan just for you. One glimpse into your future, through a moment in His presence, will be worth the pain of the process and the struggles of your past, as you boldly declare, "I am now prepared for purpose."

The Lord has lifted you to a new place. He has pulled you higher, strengthened your spirit, increased your anointing, and fueled your desire to be in His presence. You have been *Drawn to Destiny!*

Essential Spiritual Ingredients
The wisdom to wait in worship for the wind